**TO:**

_____

**FROM:**

_____

**DATE:**

_____

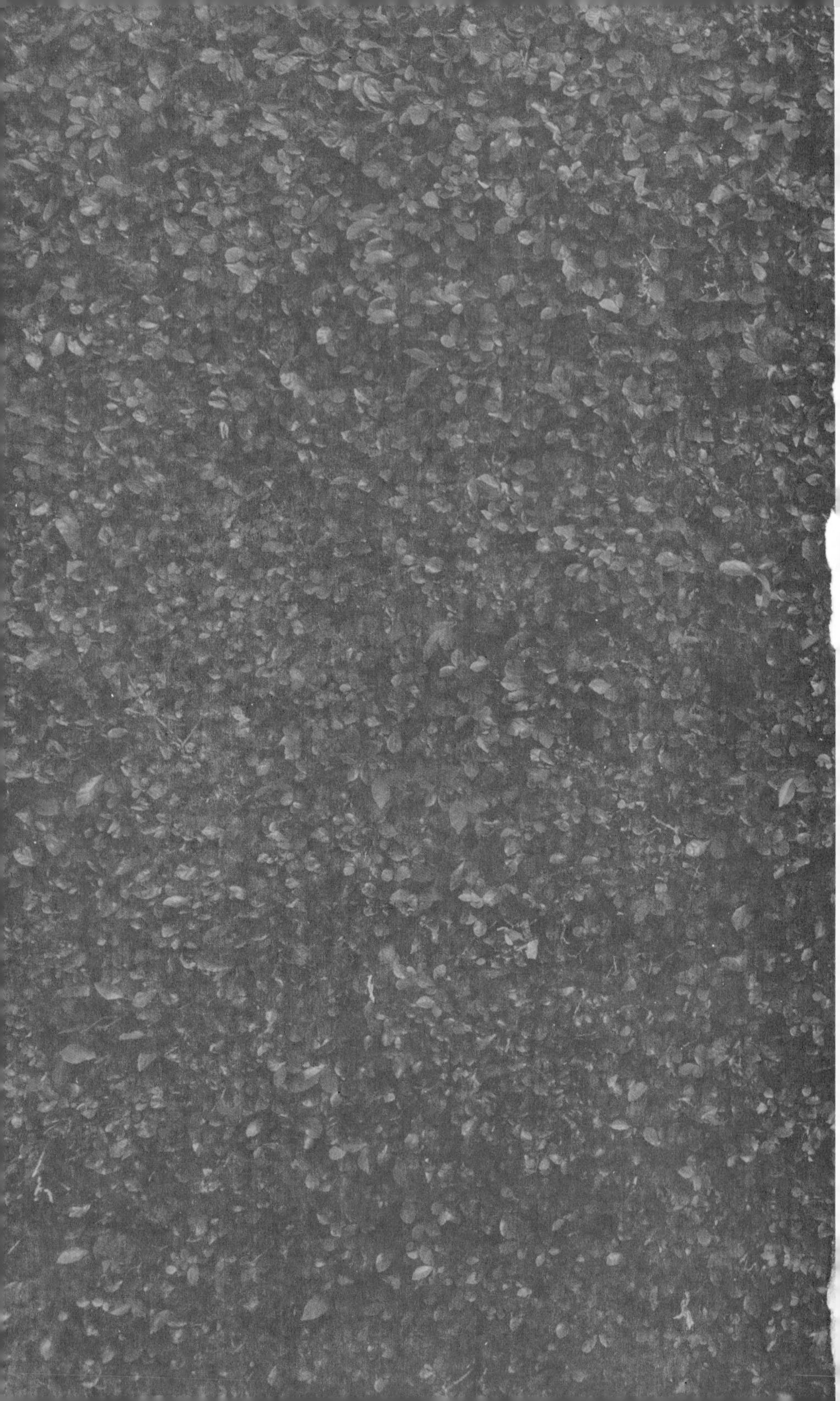

# NO WOMAN LEFT BEHIND

## GUIDED JOURNAL

A JOURNEY TO BREAKING UP WITH YOUR
FEARS AND REVOLUTIONIZING YOUR LIFE

## SARAH JAKES ROBERTS

THOMAS NELSON
Since 1798

*No Woman Left Behind Guided Journal*

© 2022 Sarah Jakes Roberts

Some of the material in this book was previously published in *Woman Evolve: Break Up with Your Fears and Revolutionize Your Life* © 2021 (Thomas Nelson).

Published in Nashville, Tennessee, by Thomas Nelson. Thomas Nelson is a registered trademark of HarperCollins Christian Publishing, Inc.

Thomas Nelson titles may be purchased in bulk for educational, business, fund-raising, or sales promotional use. For information, please email SpecialMarkets@ThomasNelson.com.

Cover photo and all photos of Sarah Jakes Roberts in this book © Brian K. Freeman Jr.

The rose line art on the cover and title page is © istockphoto.

Unless otherwise noted, Scripture quotations are taken from the New King James Version®. Copyright © 1982 by Thomas Nelson. Used by permission. All rights reserved.

Scripture quotations marked NIV are taken from the Holy Bible, New International Version®, NIV®. Copyright © 1973, 1978, 1984, 2011 by Biblica, Inc.® Used by permission of Zondervan. All rights reserved worldwide. www.zondervan.com. The "NIV" and "New International Version" are trademarks registered in the United States Patent and Trademark Office by Biblica, Inc.®

Any internet addresses, phone numbers, or company or product information printed in this book are offered as a resource and are not intended in any way to be or to imply an endorsement by Thomas Nelson, nor does Thomas Nelson vouch for the existence, content, or services of these sites, phone numbers, companies, or products beyond the life of this book.

ISBN 978-1-4002-3687-9 (HC)

*Printed in India*

22 23 24 25 26 BPI 10 9 8 7 6 5 4 3 2 1

# CONTENTS

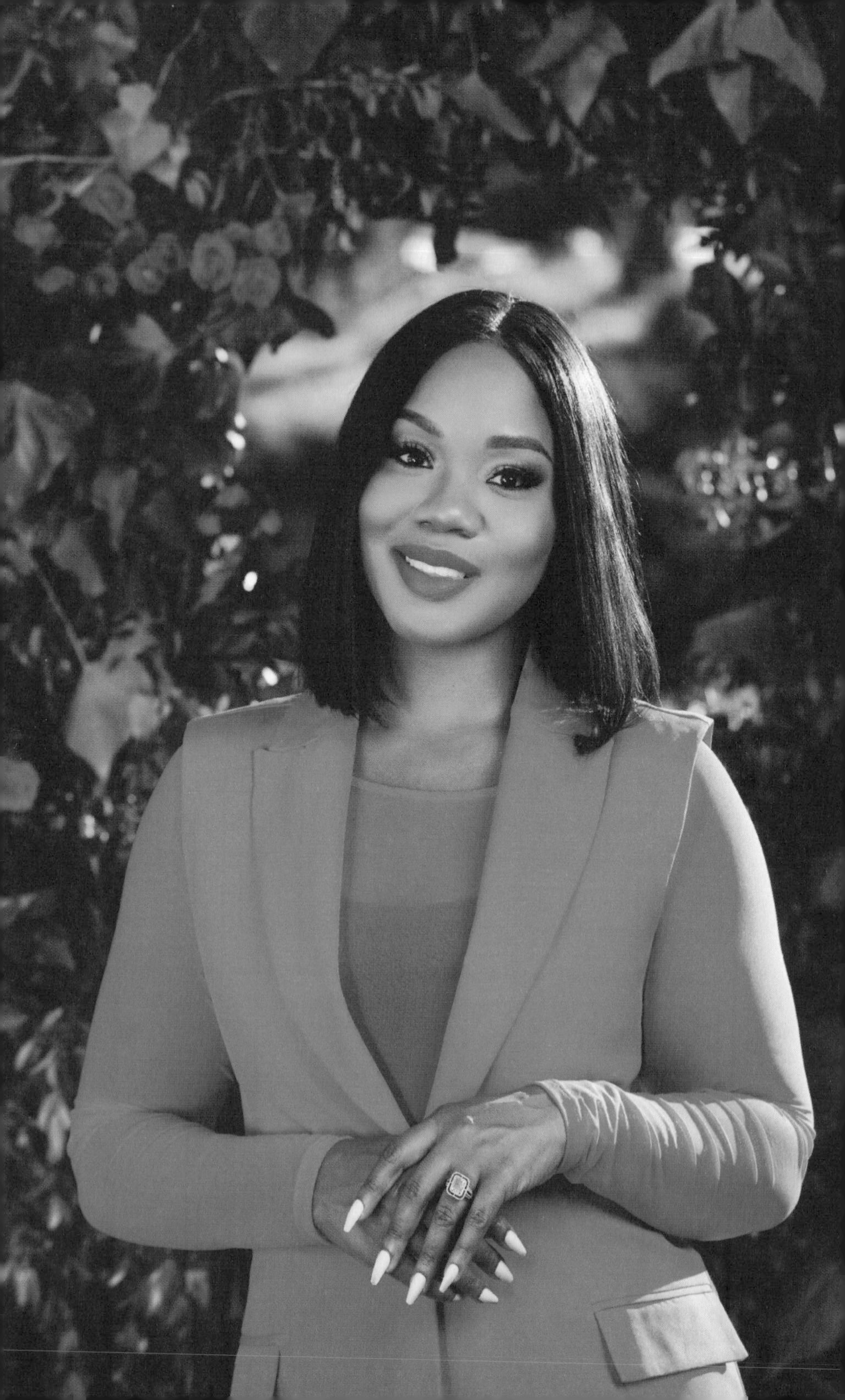

# THE
# INVITATION

Hey you,

I wish I could tell you in person how excited I am for you to be on this journey with me. The greatest gift you can give yourself and the people you're assigned to is the best, most healed version of you. This journal is going to help you do just that. We're going to spend time bringing light and clarity to how you've changed and developed over the years.

Finding time and a safe space to dive into your heart, unravel your many experiences, and discover the thoughts, hopes, and fears connected to those experiences isn't always easy. I know firsthand that those are the moments when we need to hear from someone who has been there before. I'm going to be that person for you.

Maybe you feel lost in a world that seems bigger than you. Or maybe you're attempting to recover after a setback. Or you may be ready to bring forth good fruit despite the forbidden fruit to which you were exposed. I want to help

5

you grow from where you are today to the place God has marked as your finish line. And this journal is where we are buckling down together to move forward in faith and hope. In these pages I'm inviting you to bravely look at what you've endured, where you may be stuck today, and who God is calling you to be.

I created this guide for one person: *you.*

I designed it to help you evolve. In *Woman Evolve,* I share my own journey to becoming the woman God created me to be, and I crafted this journal to equip *you* to become the version of you that God created to revolutionize the world. Both are based on what God has shown me and on the freedom countless other women in the *Woman Evolve* movement are experiencing.

This journal is for your eyes only, so I want you to keep it real here! If you're tempted to fudge a little as you write in these pages—to hold back some of your mess, to omit some of your crazy, to avoid some of your sin—then this journey may not be for you. When you "filter" the reality of your life, you do a disservice to *yourself.* (Because—trust!—God *knows.*) There's no one here you need to impress.

I also want to encourage you to take your time. There are no prizes for rushing through this process. No extra credit for being the first one to finish. *Go slow.* If you find yourself stuck on a question or idea, pause there and invite the Holy Spirit to help you understand *why* you're stuck. And then *listen.*

Finally, sometimes we look at moments in our history

as small or inconsequential compared to the things other people face, but when something wounds you, it doesn't matter whether it would've wounded someone else. It's not wise to compare or minimize our pain because it doesn't feel significant compared to that of others. When we do this, we run the risk of not recognizing the moment that destabilized our confidence and identity. So don't minimize the moment that impacted your heart.

If you are truly ready to break up with your fears and revolutionize your life, then gather your courage and let's take this ride together.

*Sarah*

PS This moment in your life, this season in your journey, is *unique*. And that means that what God is transforming in you right now isn't what God healed five years ago and it's not what God will redeem ten years from now. So I encourage you to jot down the date you are beginning this particular transformational journey:

[Month] _January_ [Day] _27_ [Year] _2024_

(When you testify about how God brought peace, confidence, and clarity to your soul, you're going to want to remember this day!)

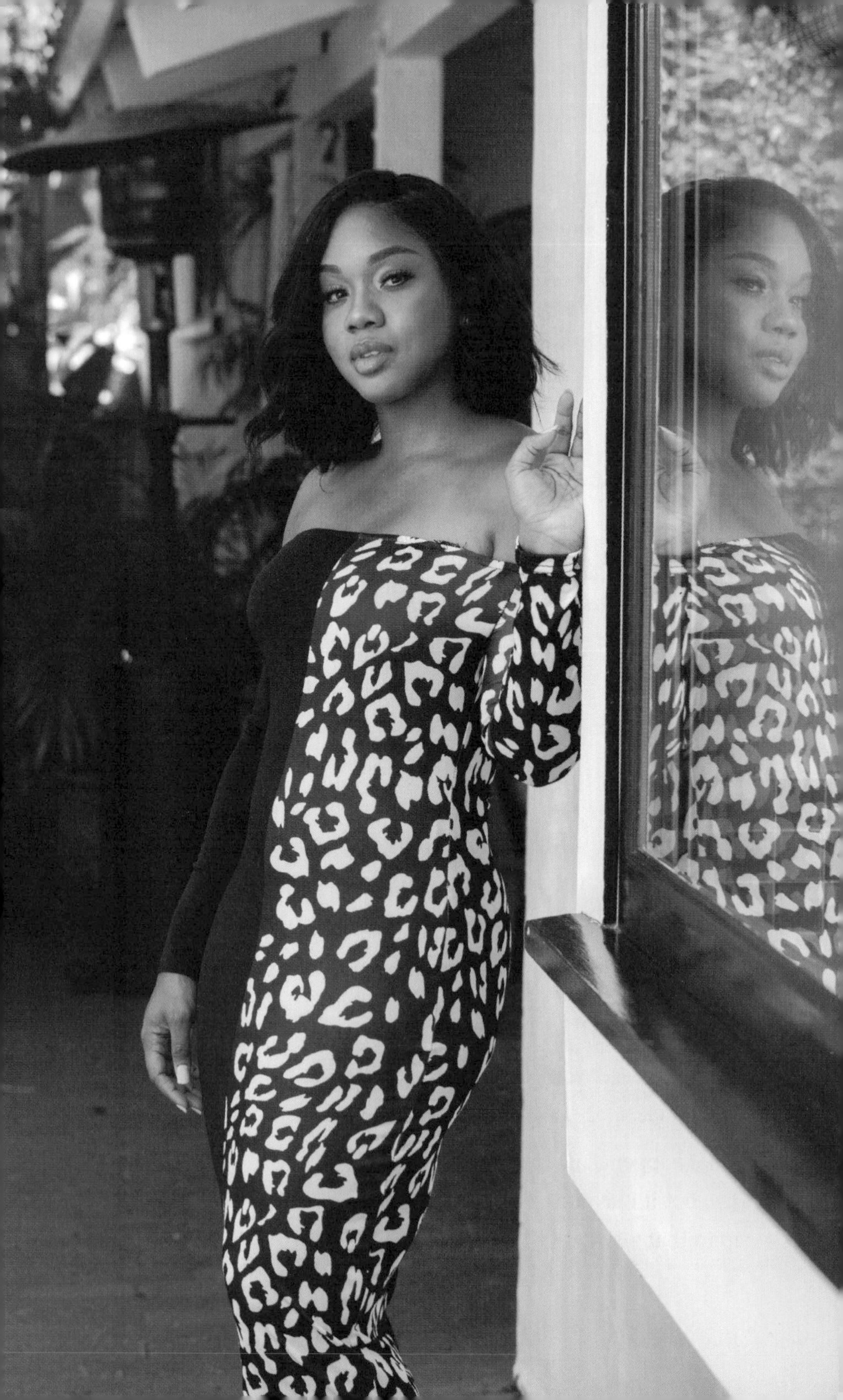

# CHAPTER ONE

# RESCUE EVE

> *Then God blessed them, and God said to them,*
> *"Be fruitful and multiply; fill the earth and subdue*
> *it; have dominion over the fish of the sea, over the*
> *birds of the air, and over every living thing that*
> *moves on the earth."*
> —GENESIS 1:28

It's hard to remember that Eve's story didn't begin the moment she ate from the forbidden fruit. Over time her identity has become synonymous with her most shameful moment. Maybe you can relate? I know I can. God's vision for Eve's identity versus the identity that her experiences placed on her are completely different. In God's plan Eve was blessed, capable of producing fruit, filling the earth, and having dominion. What happened in the garden did not change God's vision for Eve, but it may have changed whether Eve felt she could live up to that vision.

The tragedy of the garden is not just that Eve ate from the tree but that Eve's action produced (and multiplied) a distrust of God and then herself. We're thousands of years away from that fateful moment in the garden, yet almost every woman I know has had to wrestle with that same distrust. I've struggled to trust that God's love, grace, and mercy still extends to me, and I've struggled to trust my own decision-making. Eve knew before she ate from the tree that it would lead to death. Her heart continued to beat, but her confidence, vulnerability, and peace quickly began to fade. God didn't leave her without a road map that could resurrect her divine identity, but my girl, Eve, and my girl holding this journal would have to be willing to do the work.

That work begins with our choices. Every day we are given many opportunities to choose what we know is good and right for us. But if you're like me, there are times throughout the day when my discipline to do what I know is good and right is overshadowed by the temptation to do what I know will ultimately slow my progress. In other words, you know what it's like to know better but not do better. Maybe you're like me, and you "closet eat" french fries in the car before you get home with everyone's dinner. Or you overindulge and buy things you know you don't need (but convince yourself you really do). No doubt we all stalk the social-media pages of those who have hurt us, allowing our thoughts of shame, anger, fear, anxiety, insecurity, and doubt to take the mic—sometimes to the point we no longer have the faith required to live life with integrity or confidence. In those moments, when we choose to resist what we know we should do, we are subconsciously also choosing to live inwardly unfulfilled, envious, and apprehensive; in toxic relationships; and addicted, stressed, depressed, and/or ashamed of ourselves . . . The list goes on and on, but all of it ends in a state of devastation. The truth is that no matter how easy people may make it seem, it can be incredibly challenging to abandon toxic habits and instead choose to do what we know is right.

## GET REAL ABOUT WHERE YOU'RE STUCK

As we begin, I want you to pause and consider the small and large ways *you've* chosen a path that has diverted you from the commitments and goals you have for yourself. Maybe it was a single momentary lapse in judgment. Or it might be a chronic season of making poor choices. (Those fries aren't going to eat themselves, after all.) Or perhaps there's an underlying fear that is keeping you from moving forward.

Ask God to help you see what you need to see.

------

*Pray: Spirit, open the eyes of my heart to show me the places where I've been thwarting the goodness You have for me. Speak, Lord, Your servant is listening.*

------

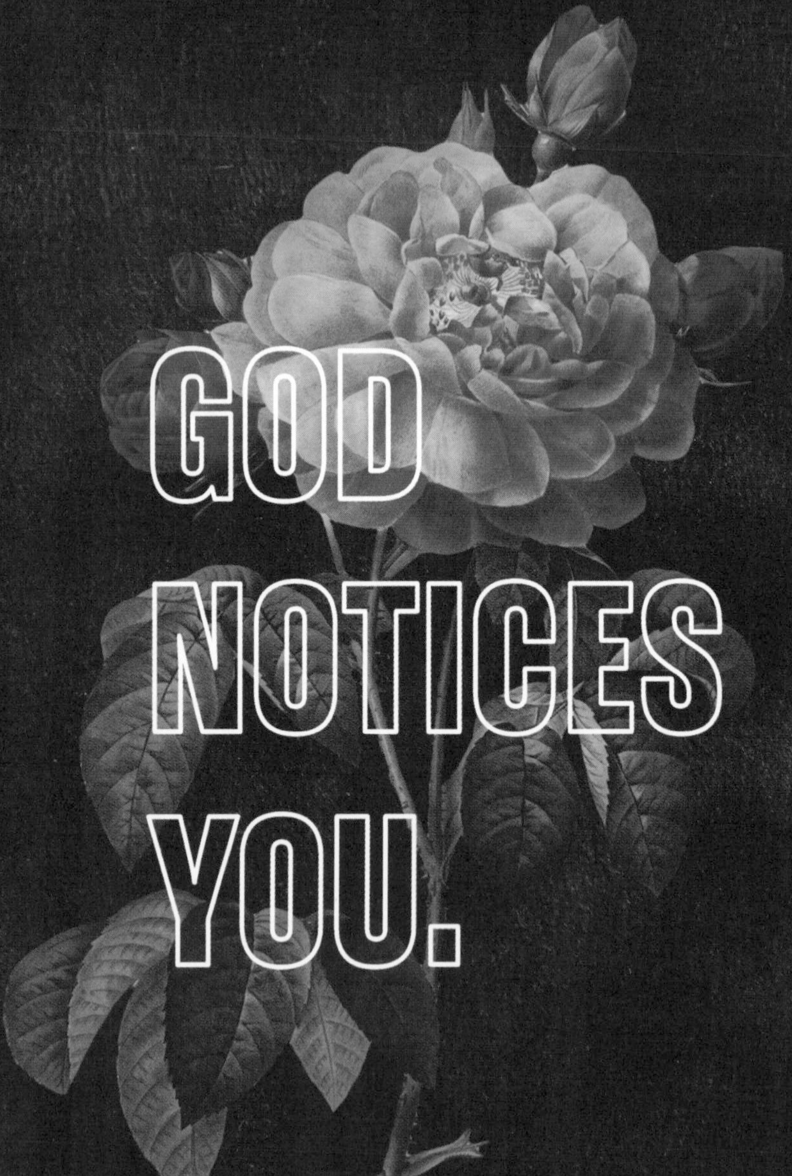
GOD
NOTICES
YOU.

*A character goal is one that you set for your personal behavior, based on your faith.*

A *character* goal I have for myself is _____
_____,
but I've made the following choice(s) that has compromised
that goal:

_____

_____

_____

_____

*A spiritual goal is one you set for your relationship with God.*

A *spiritual* goal I have for myself is to be who God
wants me to be _____,
but I've made the following choice(s) that has compromised
that goal:

not being committed to him and
focusing on the things he showe
me,

_____

_____

*A financial goal is one you set to work toward financial stability or prosperity.*

A *financial* goal I have for myself is <u>to Save money</u>
_____ ,

but I've made the following choice(s) that has compromised that goal:

<u>eating out unnecessary spending</u>

_____

_____

_____

*A physical goal is one you set for your physical body—often involving diet, rest, or exercise.*

A *physical* goal I have for myself is <u>Confidence,</u>
<u>Committed</u> ,

but I've made the following choice(s) that has compromised that goal:

<u>I get in my own head Great Start</u>
<u>When i see little results I give up</u>
<u>and be okay with what I see</u>

_____

_____

*A relational goal is one you set to improve your relationships with others.*

A *relational* goal I have for myself is _being friends_
_and opning up to peple_ ,
but I've made the following choice(s) that has compromised that goal:

_not going places to meet new_
_peple not tuking the time for_
_myself_

_____

*An emotional goal is one you set to care for your emotional well-being.*

An *emotional* goal I have for myself is _Caring_
_What other think_ ,
but I've made the following choice(s) that has compromised that goal:

_allowing others to dictate how_
_my day will be._

_____

_____

_____

*A professional goal is one you set to move forward in your career.*

A *professional* goal I have for myself is _____

_____,

but I've made the following choice(s) that has compromised that goal:

_____

_____

_____

_____

Note: Okay, so listen, taking the time to look at all the areas where you've compromised your goals can leave you feeling naked, but don't be ashamed. That's the point, friend. This is a judgment-free zone. There's not a person on this planet who doesn't have room to grow and become better. I know this inventory wasn't easy, friend. I'm proud of you for digging in!

## IT DIDN'T START WITH FRUIT

When God asked Eve why she ate from the fruit, she told God that the Serpent deceived her and then she ate. The Serpent had to uproot her truth before he could plant the insecurity that led to her deterioration. Can you remember the first time your truth was uprooted? Can you remember the first time you no longer felt safe? Loved? Wanted? Liked? Good enough? Beautiful? Innocent? Can you remember how it made you question yourself and others?

This is deep work, isn't it? And it's *important* work. Quiet your heart before God, and begin at your birth and the context in which you were born, noticing the events—year by year—that may have threatened your sense of

- trusting God's plan for your life,
- physical or emotional safety,
- being loved,
- being wanted,
- being liked,
- being good enough,
- being beautiful, or
- being innocent.

You may come upon one or more major traumas. Something may pop into your mind that you never considered to be very significant. And you may even recall a memory that's been buried for years. Each one matters, big and small, so without any judgment, prepare to write them down.

> ### A Note from Sarah
>
> Friend, God *notices* you. And God grieves every experience of pain and trauma you endured. Because He has a master plan for your life, for your good and not your harm, know that He is redeeming your suffering.

Note, here, any life events that may have ruptured the security and confidence God intended for you to enjoy.

*People telling me that I'm not Good enough or just not believing in myself that I am worthy.*

## LISTEN FOR THE ROOT QUESTION

As you consider the life events you noted above, ask God to show you which one was the most *transformational* in your becoming who you are today. Where's the sticky spot? When were you wounded?

The most transformational event—impacting my sense of who I am, and making me feel less valuable—in my early life was:

My looks

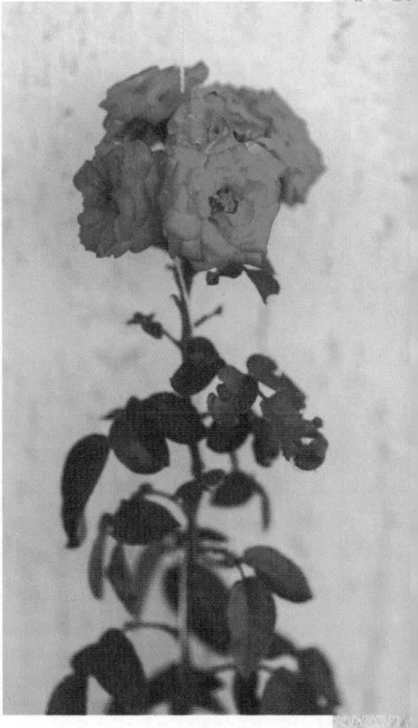

If it's unresolved, then this event continues to impact your life today in your health, your relationships, your career, your habits, your choices, and so on. Think about *one* area of your life that is most impacted by this event. You will need this to help you in the next chapter.

The area of my life today in which I'm most affected by this event:

_What did I do wrong_

_____

_____

_____

_____

_____

The seed of trauma begins as a question. It did for Eve, and it does for us. As you consider the event you noted above, what was the root question that was planted in your heart by that event? What is the question that haunts you? What is it that finds a way to creep into the most unsuspecting moments of your life? That question is a seed that if not properly addressed will continue to control your actions.

For one woman the root question was, *Are you really worth loving?* Another heard, *Are you enough?* For me the root question was, *Do you really belong here?* Yours may be different.

What is the root question that continues to haunt your heart? Note it here.

Why they dont like me or love me Why they cant be happy for me they are against me.

The insatiable need to answer that question about our identity leads us to forbidden fruit. And it's that question that God wants to finally lay to rest on this journey we're taking.

How did that pivotal event, and the question it elicited, impact the choices you've made? (In your relationship to God, to others, to yourself, to food, to money, to substances . . . to *everything*.)

I stress eat spend money I allow others to dictate my day when they make me mad

## ACCESS GOD'S HELP

As much as we may say we want to evolve, let's be honest: change can be scary. Even when we've experienced fear, shame, disappointment, and trauma, these are companions we *know*. For better or for worse, *they're familiar.*

Sis, believe me, I get it. And I want you to hear that you're not alone in this. I am with you. Other sisters on this journey are with you. And God is with you in every way. Take some time to talk to God about this journey toward freedom.

## HOW TO PRAY

Think about an image or phenomenon that reminds you that God is *real*. It might be a sunset over the ocean. It might be a pregnancy or a newborn's first cry. Call to mind that which makes your heart *certain* that God is real.

Then, as you hold the vastness of God in your consciousness, open your heart to the areas where our big God can grant you big healing, courage, guidance, and strength.

Take your time. Then note here what God is speaking to your heart.

I know you love me I know I can
be a better mother and wife I know
if something is wrong I can call on

You. In the midst of me going through anything you can help me and my family heal together. Let my husband know what him I could cry he is my everything help her with my angry, attitude change me father god Amen

## INSPIRATION

We're still at the front end of this journey together. But it's important to me that you can see where we're headed. I want you to take a peek at the vulnerable and authentic version of you that is coming forth so that you'll recognize her as she's evolving:

*She doesn't talk herself out of getting the support she needs to be free. That version of you is not ashamed of the path that has led her to where she is today. That version of you believes health is wealth, starts the business, goes back to school. That version of you spends and saves with financial stability (and overflow!) in mind. She shatters glass ceilings. That version of you is so whole that a relationship is the cherry on top, not a necessity. That version of you believes that her potential is limitless, and the sky is only another level—not a limit. She is empowered to continuously evolve because she's fascinated by how God will reveal His perfect plan and strength through her heart and hands. That version of you does not subscribe to the notion that this is exclusively a man's world, but every industry has room for a woman who is confident that she belongs wherever God sends her.*

Now read it again and underline what's speaking directly to your heart!

So what do you think about this evolved woman? She's pretty amazing, isn't she? Sis, she's *you*!

## MY PRAYER FOR YOU TODAY

*God, it is so clear that this woman is a treasure. You've allowed her to overcome despite incredible obstacles. This moment in her life, when she intentionally partners with You, will reveal what You've always known about her: she was born to be revolutionary. She's ready to offer her past, present, and future to You. She is ready to become the version of herself that You created to revolutionize the world. Shine Your light in her heart so she can see what You see, and give her the courage to become who You made her to be. Amen.*

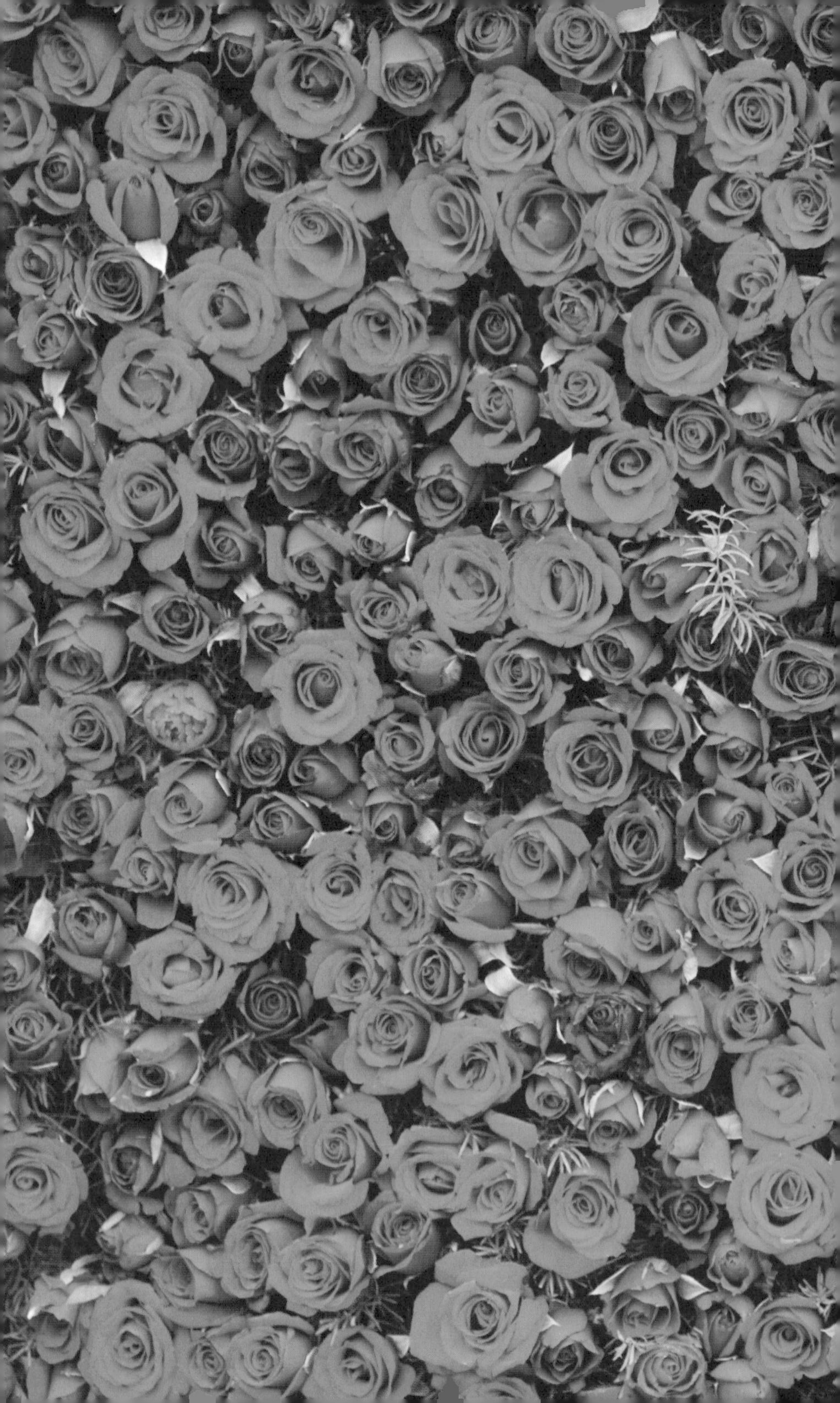

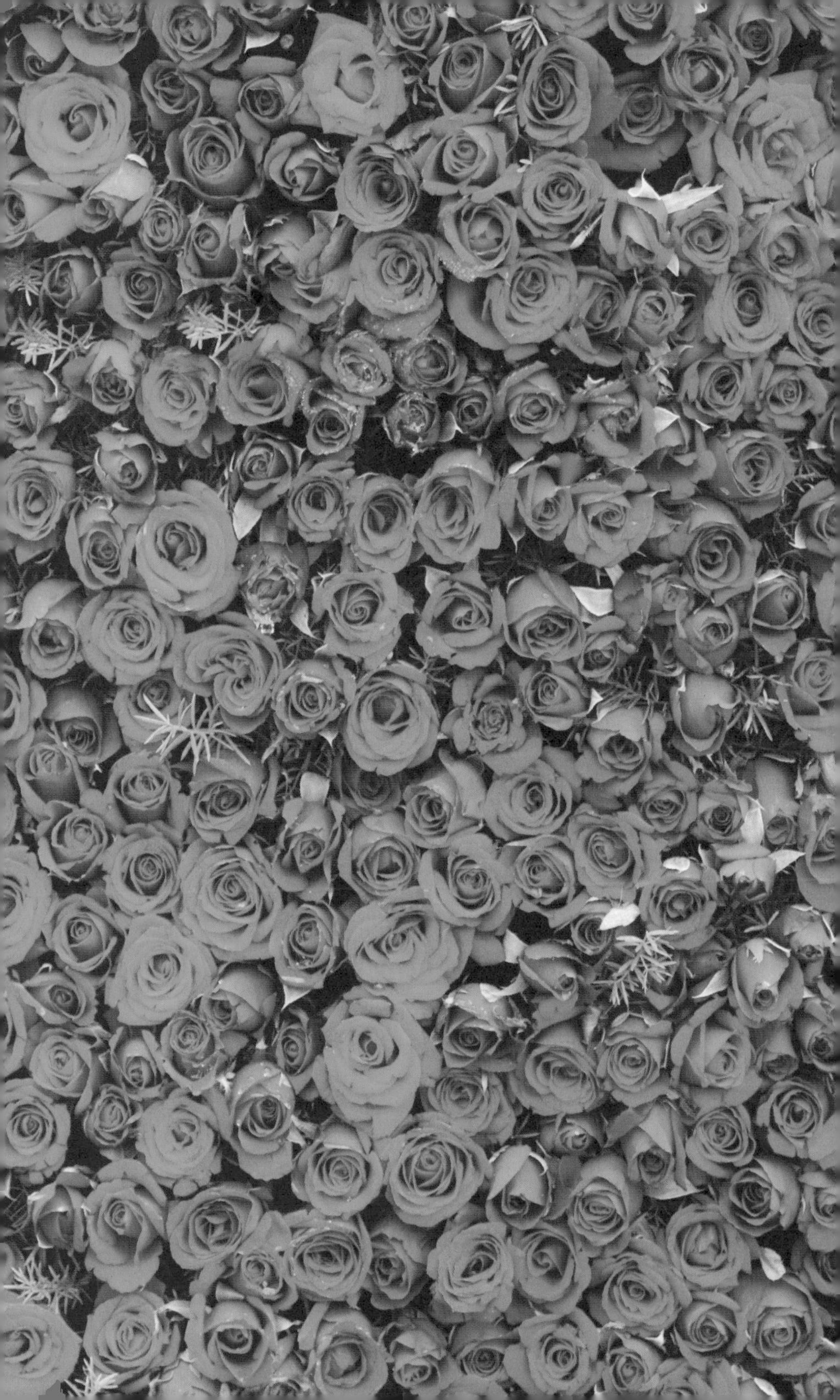

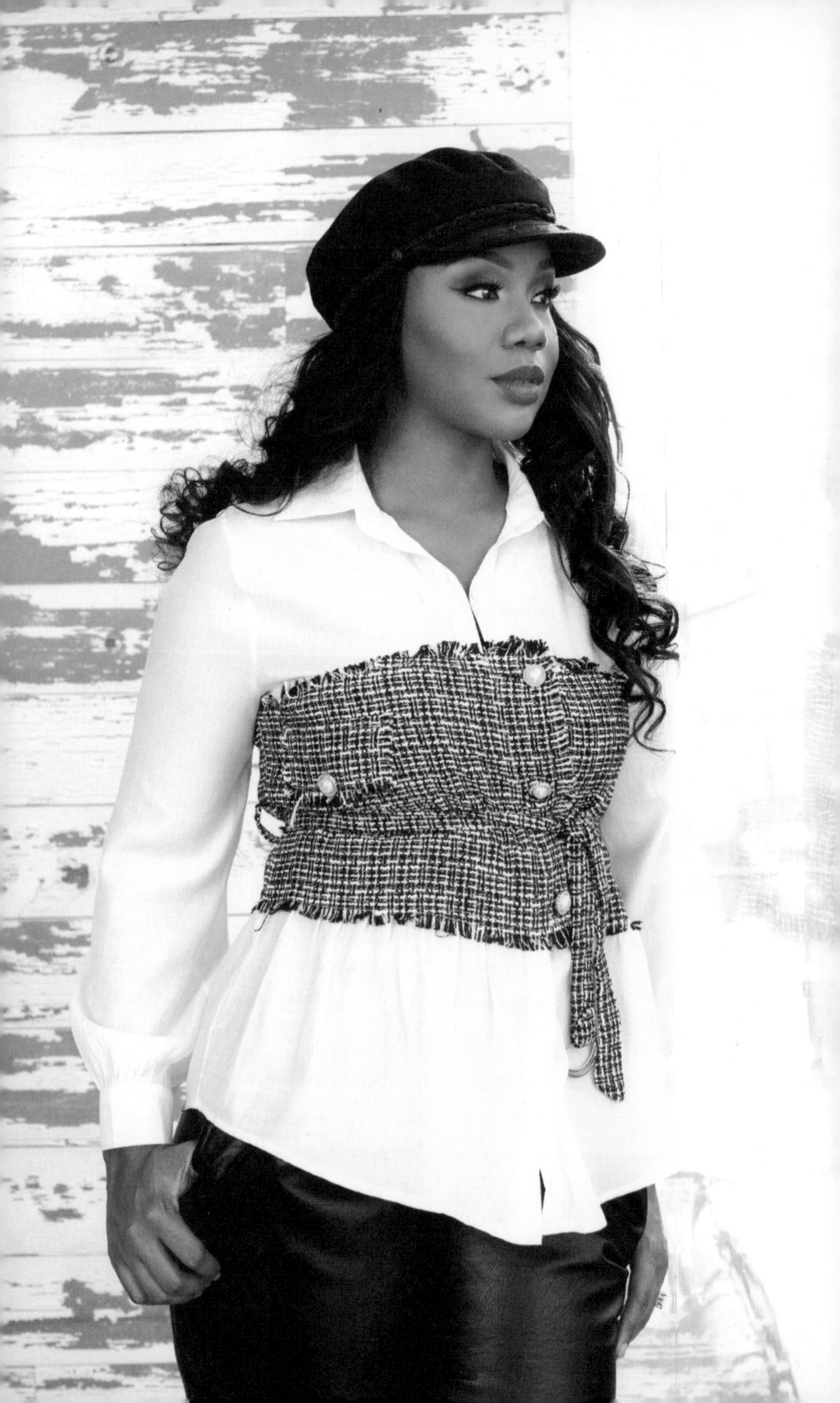

# KNOW BETTER

*Now the serpent was more cunning than any beast of the field which the LORD God had made. And he said to the woman, "Has God indeed said, 'You shall not eat of every tree of the garden'?"*
—GENESIS 3:1

Remember how I said this is a safe space? Well, sis, it's about time someone let you know you could be overweight. Before you close the book and shred our friendship contract, let me explain. I'm not talking about your body. I'm talking about your soul. What weighs us down internally are the thoughts that our fear, shame, past, and insecurities create. It's no wonder we find it difficult to reach our goals! Before we can even lock down on a plan to move forward, we must survive the mental exhaustion that comes with navigating the thoughts, emotions, and questions that come to the surface of our soul. *Will it be worth it? Do I have what it takes? Can I get it done?*

*Do I open up, or do I remain closed? Do I try again, or do I avoid the pain of disappointment? Do I stay or do I go?*

The mind becomes the arena where thoughts based in hope and optimism duel with the thoughts rooted in fear and anxiety. Each thought competes to take the lead and run our lives. We think one day the competition will reveal a winner, but in reality it's a never-ending battle until we actively intervene and make a decision.

The whirlwind of thoughts often blinds us and prevents us from recognizing that they really have only two origins: they are birthed either from our fear or from our faith. Our fears pretend to keep us safe. Our faith demands we draw on courage we aren't sure we possess.

## NOTICING THE QUESTIONS THAT SLOW YOU DOWN

In chapter 1 you identified one area of your life that you wanted to focus on in this journey to revolutionize your life. This is that area where you continue to repeat a cycle that ends with you feeling less valuable.

To keep it at the forefront of your mind and heart, write it again here:

Faith
Family
God

Sometimes we think we need to have answers to all our questions before we can move forward and make progress in that stuck area of our lives. Here are some questions that some women in your situation are asking:

*Will it be worth it?*
*Do I have what it takes?*
*Can I get it done?*
*Do I open up, or do I remain closed?*
*Do I try again, or do I avoid the pain of disappointment?*
*Do I stay, or do I go?*

When you think about this area of your life, what are the questions you think you need to answer before you can move forward? List them here:

- Why me
- how can I move forward with the pain
- Stay focus and be positive
- Let go and Let God control my mind
- Keep pushing

## PRACTICE A THERAPEUTIC BREATHING EXERCISE

The critical event you experienced became the lens through which you began to view life. Maybe you learned that trusted people abandon you. Or you might have decided that all men are dangerous. You might simply have believed that you are on your own. Now we need to take a closer look at that lens and how it impacted your view of God, yourself, and this world. So that you're in a focused, quiet space, I want to invite you into this breathing exercise to connect with what is inside you.

- Inhale like you're smelling roses, and exhale like you're blowing out a candle. (Do this three times.)
- Become one with your thoughts, emotions, and spirit, bringing them together and into focus.
- Hop into your internal time machine and drive down memory lane.
- Keep breathing.
- Go back to a moment that stands out in your mind as when you felt the most stuck. It could be ten years ago or an hour ago. Found it?
- Paint a picture in your head of your life in that moment. Who were your friends? Where were you living? How were you wearing your hair? (We always remember our hair phases.) Embody that version of yourself. Feel those fears and hopes again. Allow those bright, scary, and beautiful emotions to come back to you.
- Breathe in and breathe out as who you were then comes into focus. Now, ask yourself one simple question: *What did I need to know?* i\s okay for me to be bused i\s okay for me to let go and Let god.

As you stay in this moment, write here what it was that you needed to know. For example, in my own life, I needed to

# GOD KNOWS YOU ARE WORTHY, EVEN IF YOU DON'T SEE IT.

know I was safe. I needed to know I wasn't alone. I needed to know I was loved. I needed to know that it was okay to still have hope.

> In my own life i needed to know its okay for me to be bussed its okay for me to still have hope that God will use me the way he knows I need to be used.

- When was the first time you needed to know those things?

As you stay in this moment, noticing what it was that you needed to know, write here the first time you needed to know it. I was eight years old when I first felt my soul longing to know these things. I'd just moved from a small town to a big city and into an environment that cared more about my family name than my individuality. At that time, I needed to feel that someone saw me.

> I needed to know that God loves me and he put me here for a reason and I am worthy.

## CONNECTING THINKING, KNOWING, AND DOING

Civil rights activist, poet, and author Maya Angelou famously said, "Do the best you can until you know better. Then when you know better, do better."

I want you to begin to pay attention to what you *think*, what you *know*, and what you *do*. For instance, when I begin *thinking* I should lose weight, I work out in the morning and eat cake at night. When I start *knowing* I should lose weight, I internalize that losing weight takes work. Then I can *do*: I work out, and I cut out sugar, carbs, and fried foods from my diet. *Knowing* flips a switch that allows me to resist the temptation of living as if I don't know better.

But what about when your thoughts collide? For instance, you think you should lose weight. You also think you should eat cake! How do you determine which thought ought to be the rudder steering you forward? The thought you want to hitch your wagon to is the one that is going to help you become the woman God made you to be. That's your filter! Luke 2:52 says that Jesus "increased in wisdom and stature, and in favor with God and men." He grew stronger and healthier mentally, physically, socially, and spiritually. The thought that helps you do that is the one that should *propel* your knowing and doing.

I suspect there are some things you've known for a while. You've known that you need to get therapy. Or you've known that you need to leave that relationship. You've known that you need to take better care of your health. You've known that you need to be more disciplined with your time. You've known these things for so long that it's easier to ignore them than it is to activate and do something about them. Friend, it's not accidental that this book is in your hands: *now* is the time God has ordained for you to notice what you know so that you can *do better*.

| WHAT I THINK | WHAT I KNOW | WHAT I DO |
| --- | --- | --- |
| I should lose weight. | Losing weight takes work. | I work out and I cut out sugar, carbs, and fried foods from my diet. |
| I should go to therapy. | This is how I move forward. | I make the appointment! |

Now jot down your own *thinking, knowing,* and *doing.*

| WHAT I THINK | WHAT I KNOW | WHAT I DO |
| --- | --- | --- |
| I should lose weight | it takes time | Create healthier habits. |
| I should be open with my husband. | it could make me feel better | just talk to him |

*Knowing produces doing.* If you're not doing, then conflicting thoughts in your mind are keeping you from activating what you know.

## ACCESS GOD'S HELP

Sometimes we're not willing to know what we know. Whether it's committing to better rest, having a hard conversation with a friend, or finally applying for the degree program, we don't do what we *know* will move us closer to our goals.

Friend, God longs to be your Helper. Spend some time talking to God about beginning to do what you know by writing your prayer to Him.

- Confess the ways you've avoided *doing* what you know.
- Ask for the strength to commit to walking in a new way.
- Thank God for being your constant Helper.

Dear God . . .

I want to be free of all this sadness. I
want to love my husband the way he
deserve. I want my kids to know I
love them. I want more for myself.

## HOW TO PRAY

You know, in your head, that *knowing* leads to *doing*. And you also know that God is ready and able to help you do what is

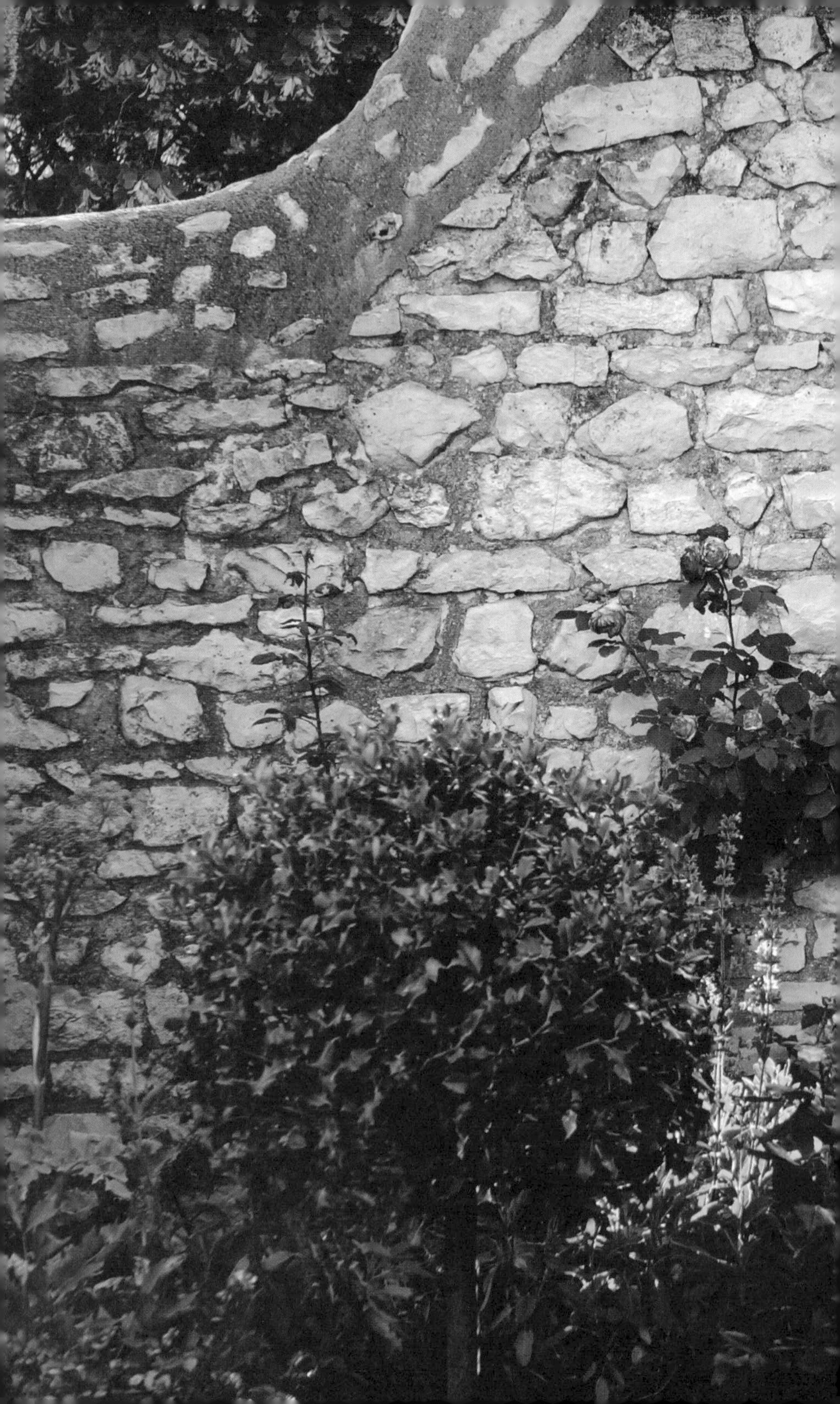

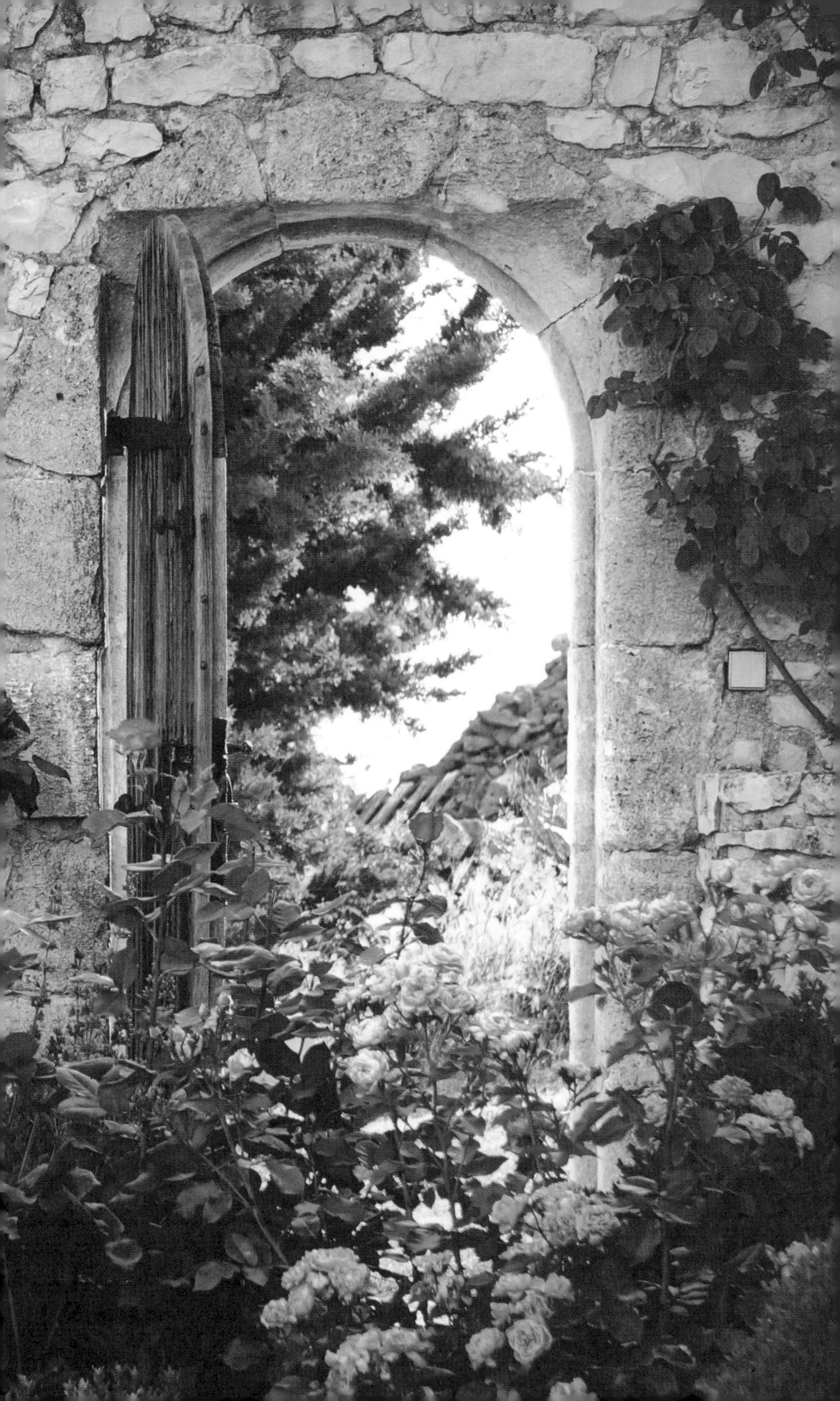

before you. God gives you everything you need to live well and be transformed.

As you pray, close your eyes and meditate on the "doing" that is before you. Whether you're facing a challenge, anticipating having a hard conversation, making a decision that requires determination, or looking at some other kind of movement or change, ask God to show you what that "doing" will look like. Let Him show you the successful resolution of what's before you. If this "doing" brings up any uncomfortable feelings, ask God to fill you with His peace that passes understanding (Philippians 4:7).

After you've spent time meditating on the "doing" to which God is calling you, note here what will be different in your life once you've taken this action.

I would let my hear go and not daubt myself and allow God to heal me and help me.

## INSPIRATION

I don't know what made you feel fragile on the inside, but I do know that before any of those things happened, God desired to partner with you on the earth. He still knows you

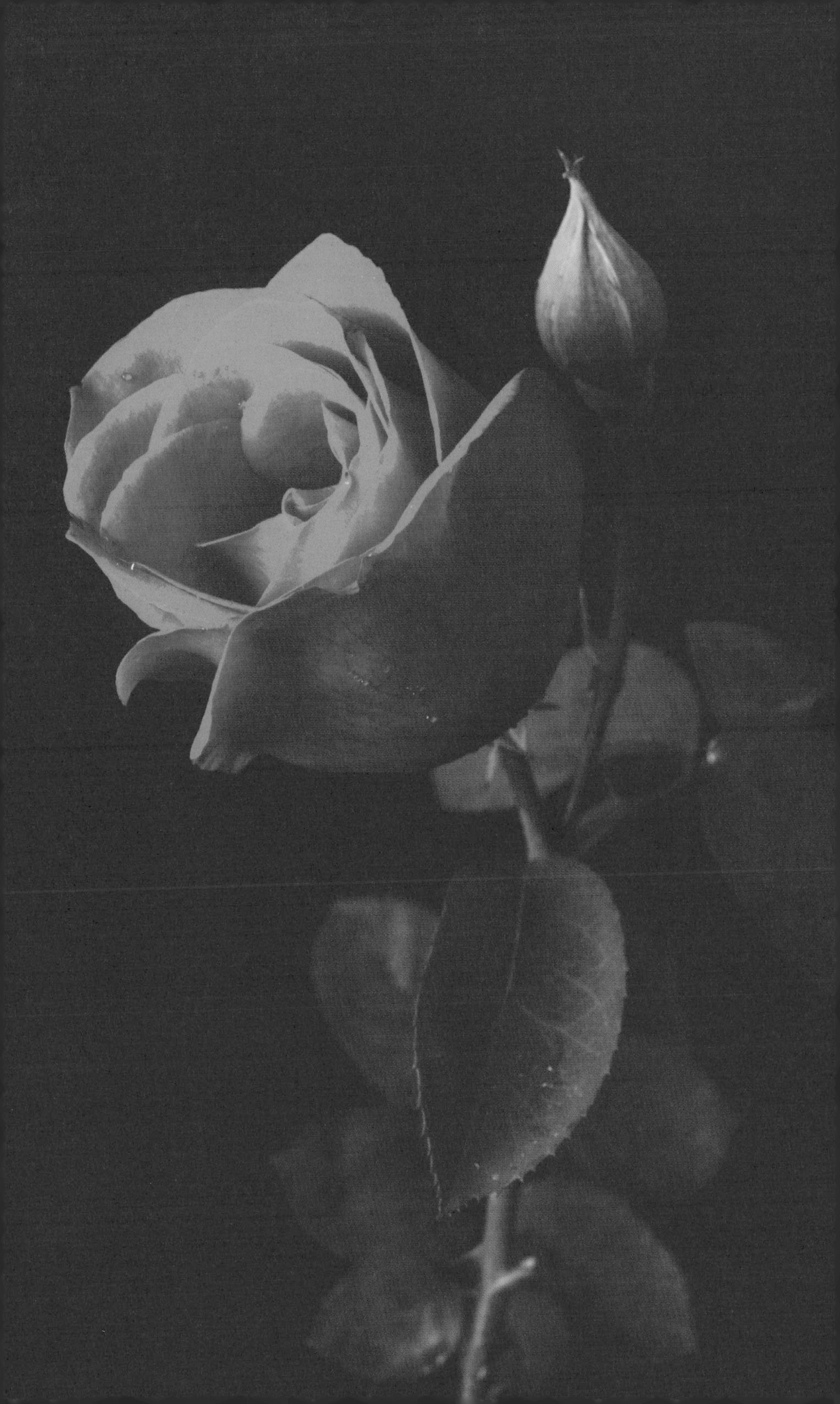

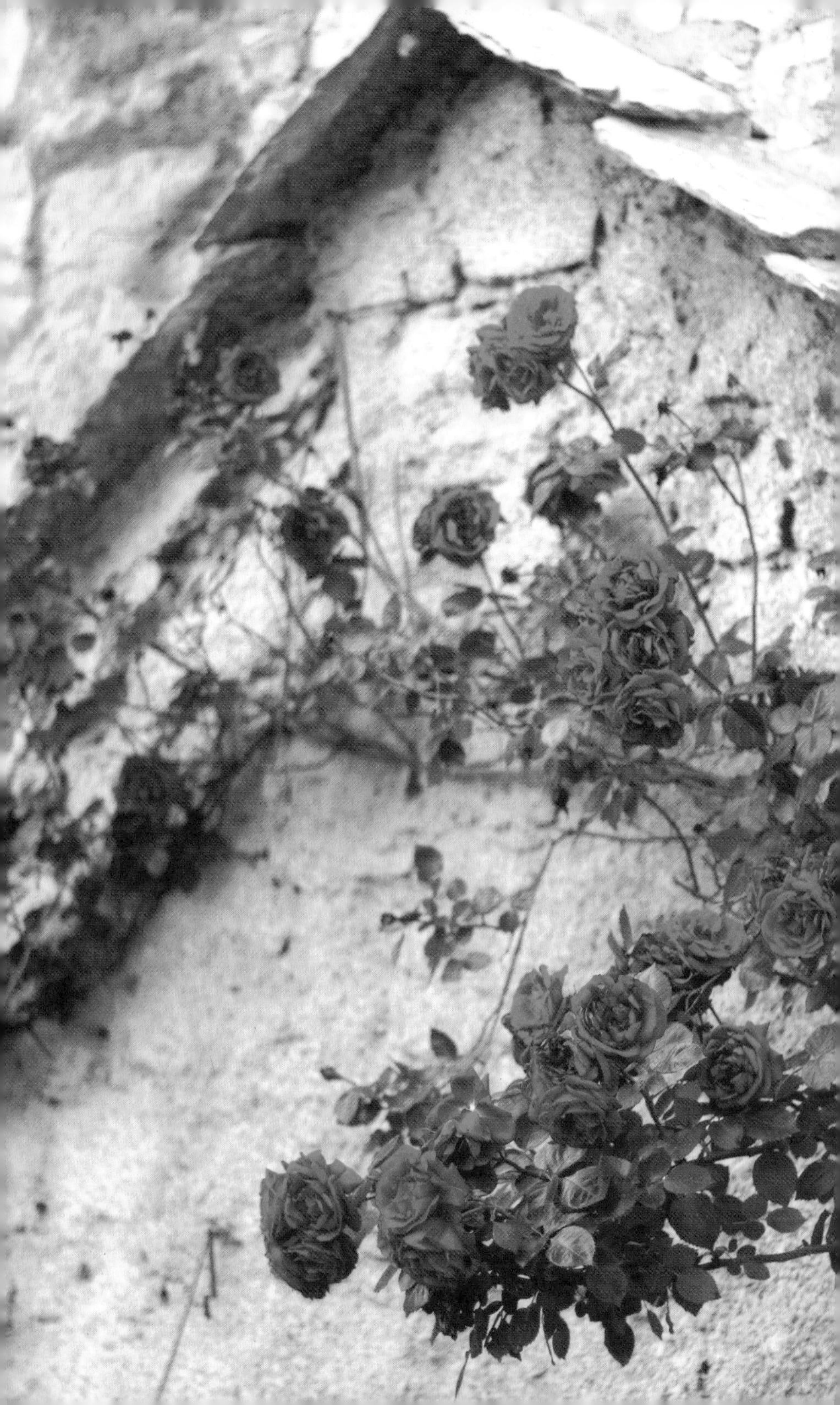

are worthy even if you don't see it. He still knows you can break generational curses and change the paradigms of your family or community culture.

In Jeremiah 29:11 God gives us insight into how much He knows about His creation: "'For I know the plans I have for you,' declares the LORD, 'plans to prosper you and not to harm you, plans to give you hope and a future'" (NIV).

Did you notice the word *know*? God told His prophet in this text that He doesn't just wonder about His plans for us; He *knows* them. The question is, do you want to discover what God knows more than you want to be stuck in what you think? Are you willing to bench your thoughts and begin pursuing what God knows? If you can commit to pursuing God, your life will have no choice but to be revolutionized.

## MY PRAYER FOR YOU TODAY

*Father God, I believe You are beginning to highlight the area of my sister's life where she has been so distracted by unprofitable thoughts that she can't activate what she knows. As she trusts You by activating what she knows, give her vision and clarity for the unknown. Amen.*

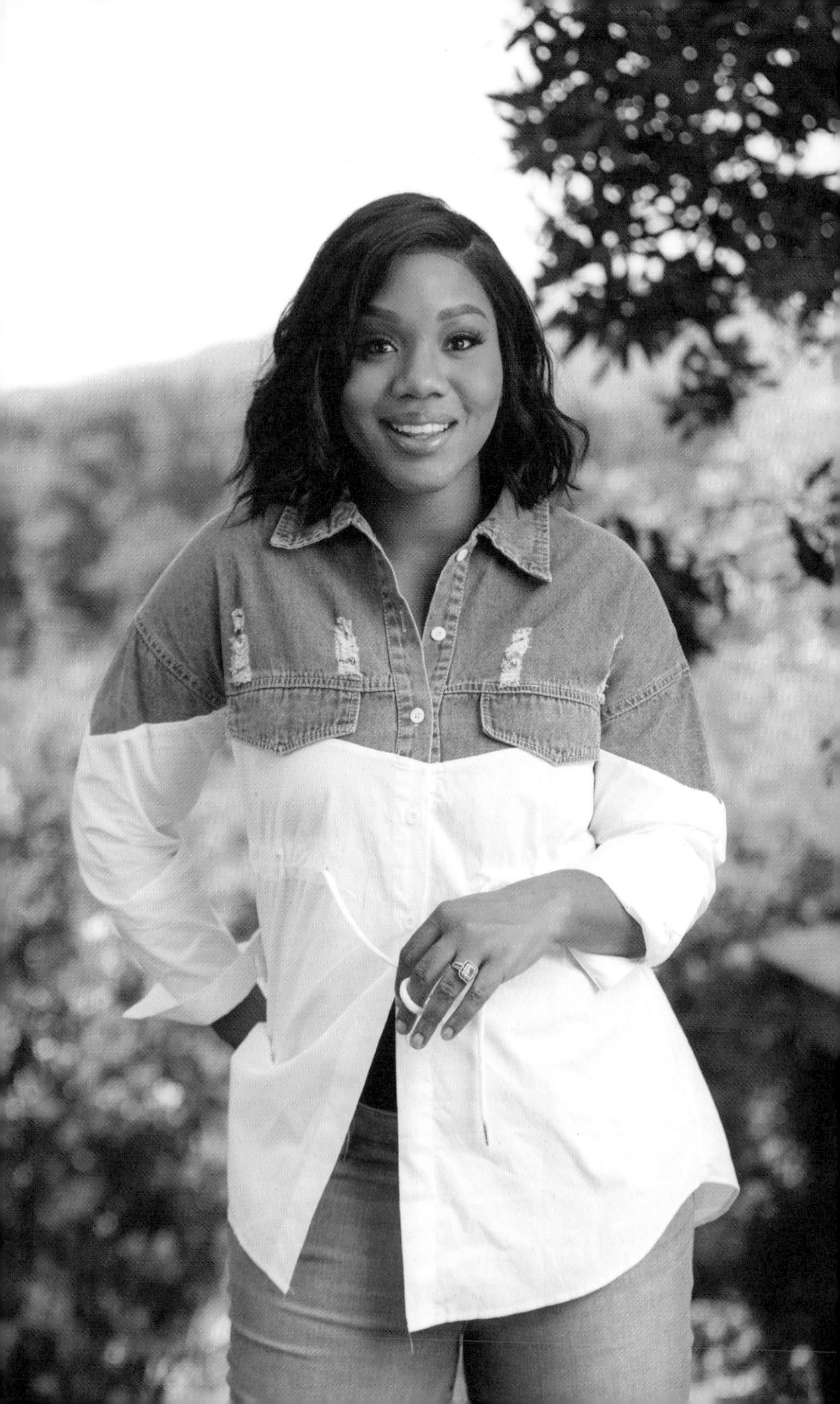

# CHAPTER THREE

# EYES WIDE OPEN

*Then the eyes of both of them were opened, and they knew that they were naked; and they sewed fig leaves together and made themselves coverings.*

—GENESIS 3:7

When Adam's and Eve's eyes were opened, they "saw" something God never wanted them to see. They were naked! But they were never supposed to see their vulnerability as something to be ashamed of.

I wonder what else we were never meant to see. That's now how I view the atrocities that have taken place in the world. I don't see them as things God allows. I see them as things God never wanted us to see. God did not intend for there to be slavery, racism, murder, hate, cancer, or death. Evil existed, as evidenced by the Serpent in the garden, but evil didn't have power over anything in its environment until Eve subjected herself to it by eating the fruit. What was done cannot be undone, but Romans 8:28 details how God can use all things to get them back to good: "And we know that all things work together for good to those who love God, to those who are the called according to His purpose." This doesn't mean that all things start as good, but that all things can get back to good with work. That's what you're doing right now. You're learning how to allow God to work in your life until He's able to look at it and be reminded of the most repeated phrase in Genesis 1: "God saw that it was good."

How, then, do we prepare ourselves for the next batch of things that are bound to come our way that we were never meant to see? You come to a place where you can control, contain, and compare what you see.

## CONTROL (AND REPLACE)

When you've subscribed to a negative narrative for a long time, changing can be hard, but it's worth it. If we want to truly strive to be like the One in whose image we've been created, we must come to a place where we commit to controlling our sight to protect our identity. You have to be willing to see yourself as more than your past. I finally did that when I started listening to that voice inside me that would nudge me

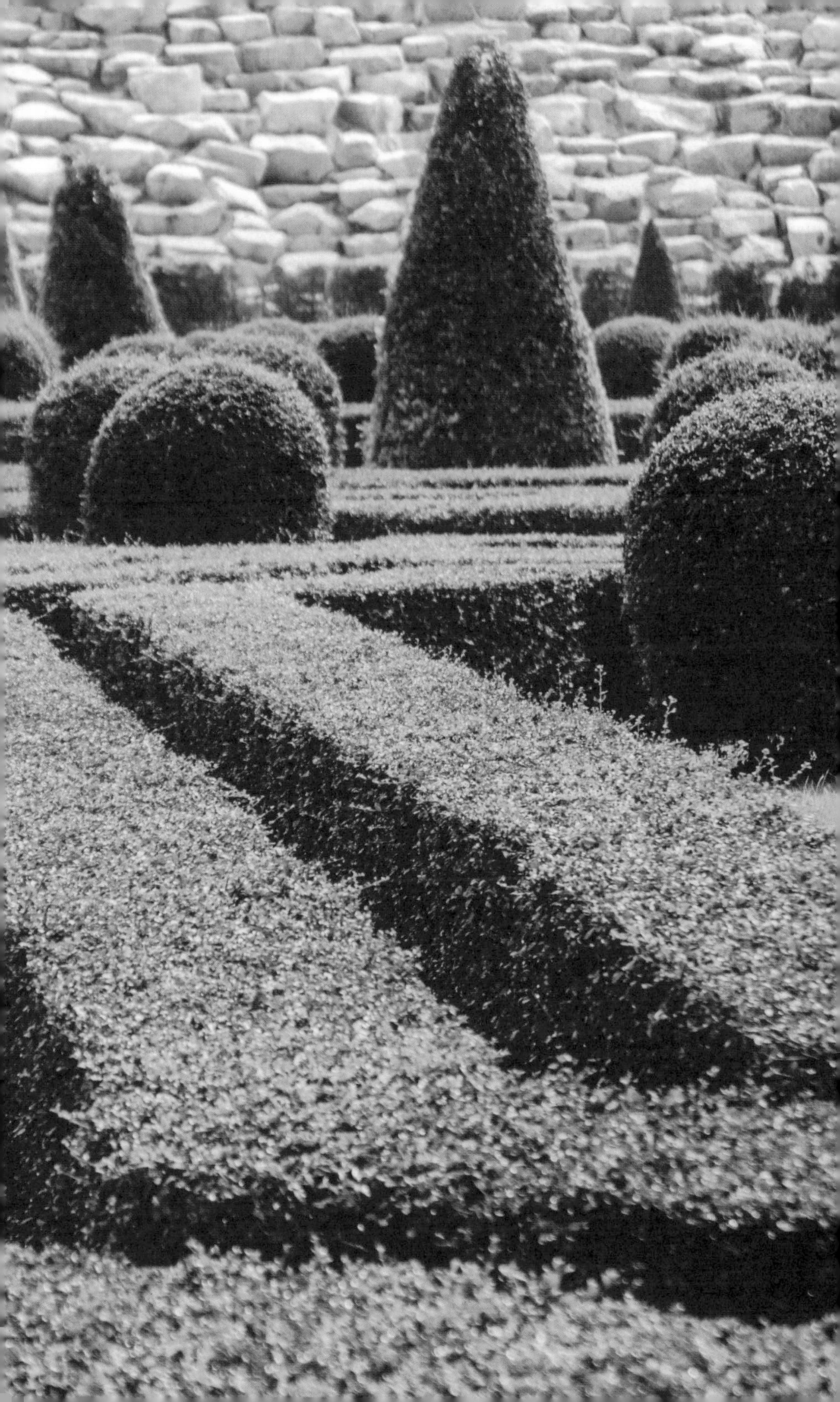

when I was looking at something I shouldn't. You are able to move forward when you replace what you *were* seeing with images that motivate you to be the woman God had in mind when you were formed.

What do you want to see in your life that you currently don't see? Hint: Focus on who you want to become rather than what you want to have.

_____

_____

_____

_____

_____

How will you achieve that goal? Hint: This feeling is a seed that helps you get closer to producing the tangible fruit!

_____

_____

_____

_____

What's keeping you from achieving that goal? Hint: Sometimes achieving your goal seems like it takes more than you have to give. You don't have the motivation, energy, faith, or discipline to radically transform your life all at once. Of course not. No one does.

---------------------------------------------

---------------------------------------------

---------------------------------------------

---------------------------------------------

---------------------------------------------

## CONTAIN (AND EMBRACE)

Containing our thoughts and emotions is not the same as repressing them. Containing our emotions is an opportunity to have self-intimacy. That's when we move from just containing to embracing.

Ask yourself, *What good could come of this?* When you go beyond containing and into embracing by playing out how what hurt you could potentially work to make you better, you exercise the divine power in you. From there, God breathes on it and takes

### A Note from Sarah

Here's the rhythm we're activating in your life:

Control the negative narrative by stopping it in its tracks.

Replace the negative narrative with a higher thought of the beauty God created when He made you.

it to the realm of "exceedingly abundantly above all that we ask or think" (Ephesians 3:20). Then one day you'll look up and be able to embrace what you didn't want to see because you're now able to contain it properly.

Journal on this: *What good could come of this?*

_____

_____

_____

_____

_____

## COMPARE (AND RELEASE)

### A Note from Sarah

The question you just journaled about isn't one you ask yourself when first confronted with your trauma. This is a question that should be reserved for when you dare to peek beyond where you are and begin to question where you could be headed.

In a social-media age it's increasingly easier to fall into the trap of comparing your life with others'. For this section I want to give you permission to compare. There's a hook though: comparing what you see has nothing to do with looking at the lives of the people around you and everything to do with daring

BE WILLING TO SEE YOURSELF

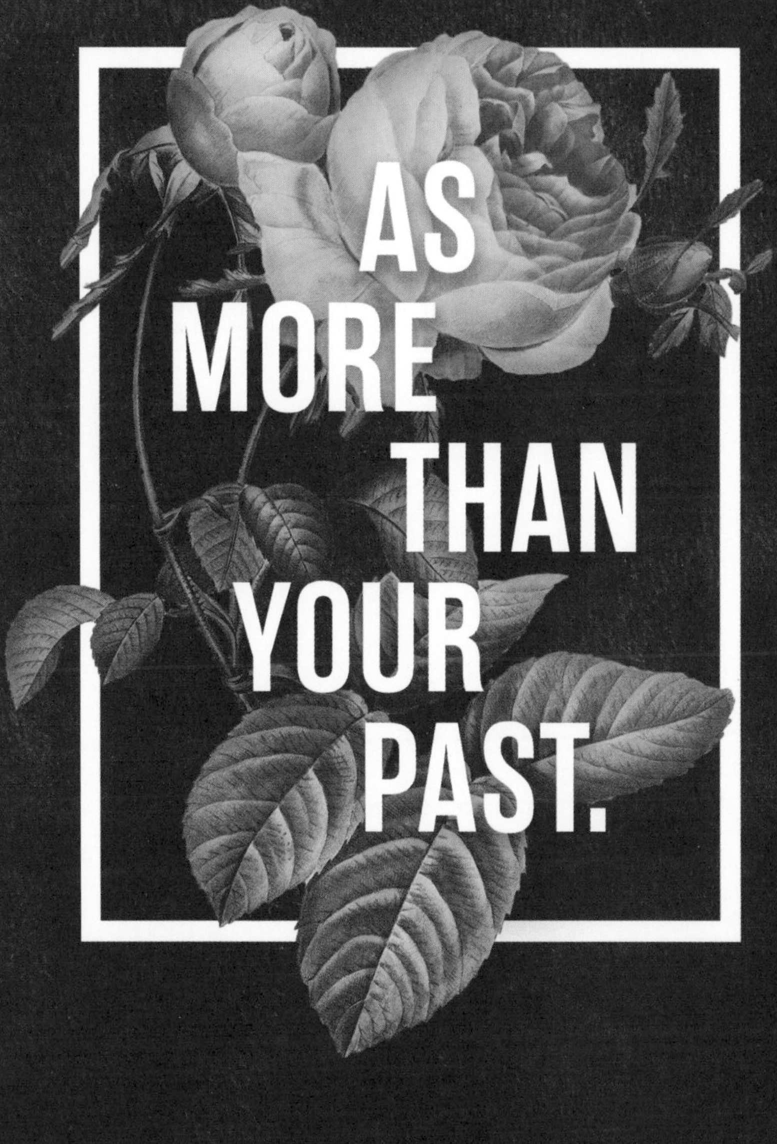
AS
MORE
THAN
YOUR
PAST.

to see your life the way God does. The ultimate goal is for you to come to a place where you can see people, circumstances, and opportunities the way that God sees them. Comparing what you see comes down to stretching your faith to look beyond your perspective on your situation and circumstance and daring to ask God to show you what He sees.

*If You're Looking at a Person Today*

God, when You see _____ (person's name here), what do You see?

_____

_____

_____

_____

_____

*If You're Looking at an Opportunity Today*

God, who will I have to become in order to pursue this opportunity? And is that version of me closer to or farther away from who I'm supposed to be in You?

_____

_____

_____

_____

_____

In the garden Jesus released what He saw for what the Father saw. Whether you're considering an opportunity or a person today, pause to pray and ask God to help you release what *you see.*

**God, I release what I see to You . . .**

_____

_____

_____

_____

_____

## ACCESS GOD'S HELP

When you set your heart to control and replace, contain and embrace, compare and release, you're on your way to finding freedom. This is holy work, and you are not in it alone.

Spend some time talking to God about what each of these looks like in your life.

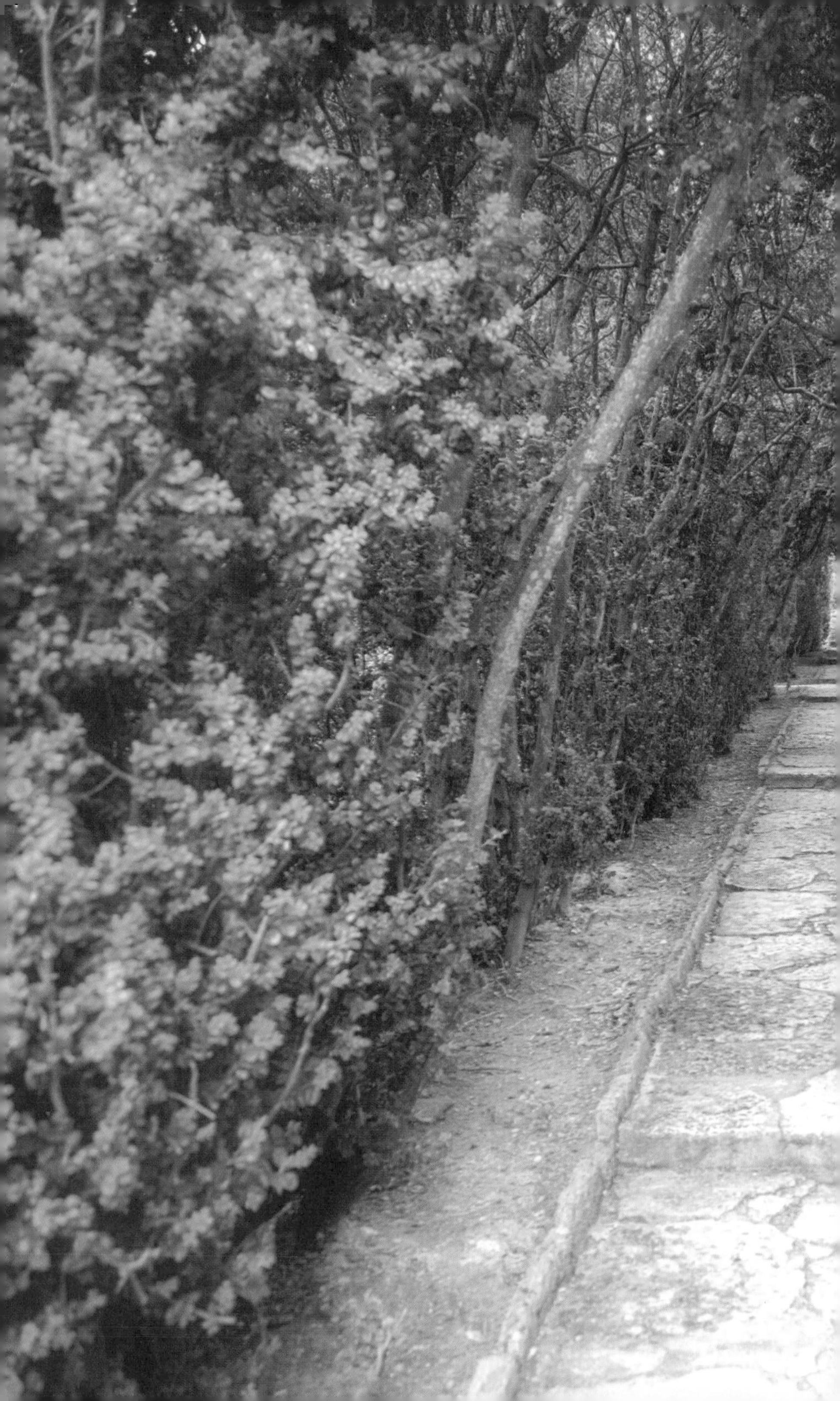

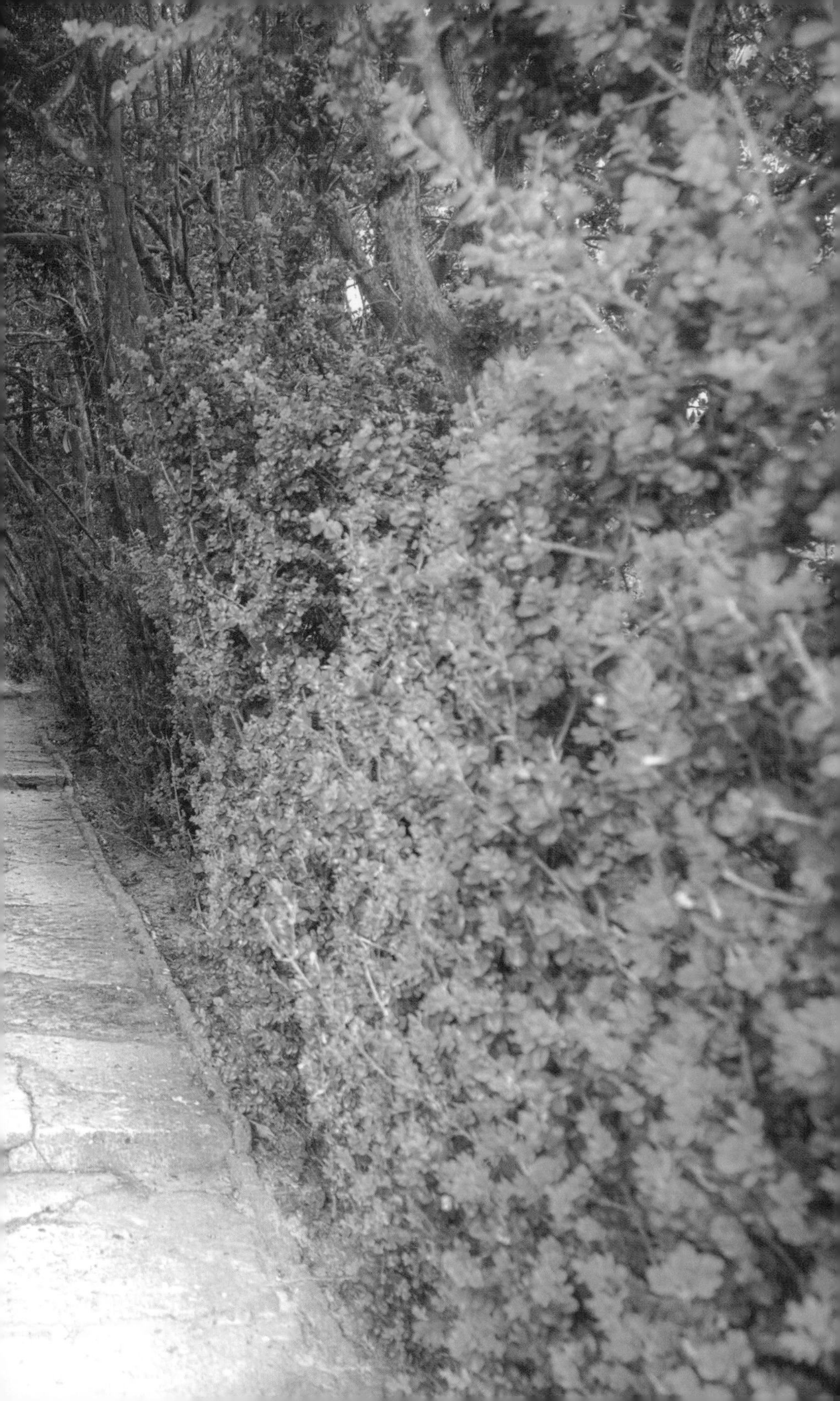

# HOW TO PRAY

A big part of the process of God's redemption is letting go of the old and embracing the new (2 Corinthians 5:17). God is a part of that process, but you also need to be an active participant.

Close your eyes and think about what's inside of you that is the "old":

- the negative narrative you've believed for too long
- the "stuckness" you feel when you replay what hurt you
- the unhelpful way you've been viewing a person or an opportunity

Ask God to show you a picture of how He is calling you to let go of what is old and embrace what is new. Then quiet your heart and notice what you see with the eyes of your heart.

Take your time. Then note here what God is speaking to your heart.

_____

_____

_____

_____

_____

_____

_____

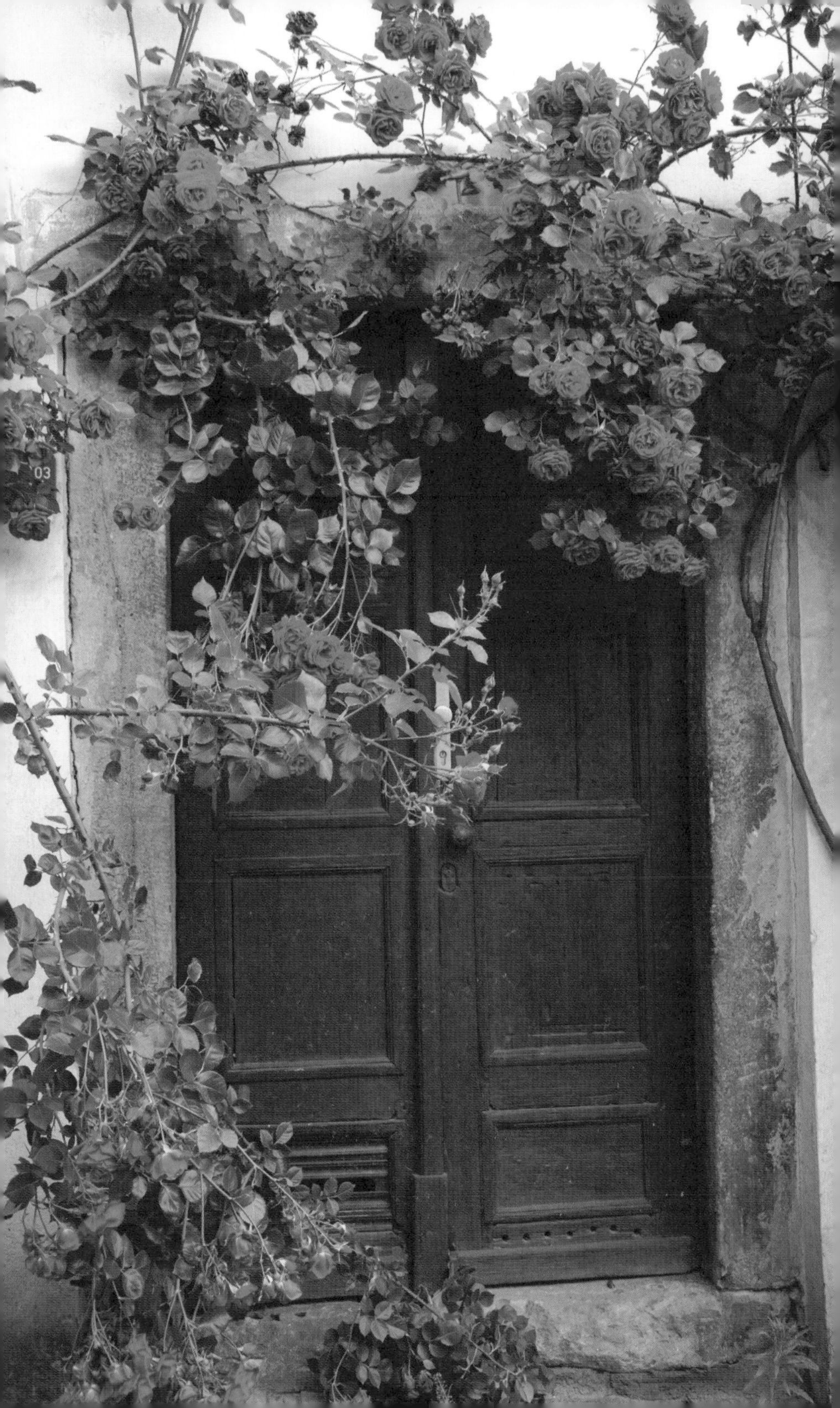
03

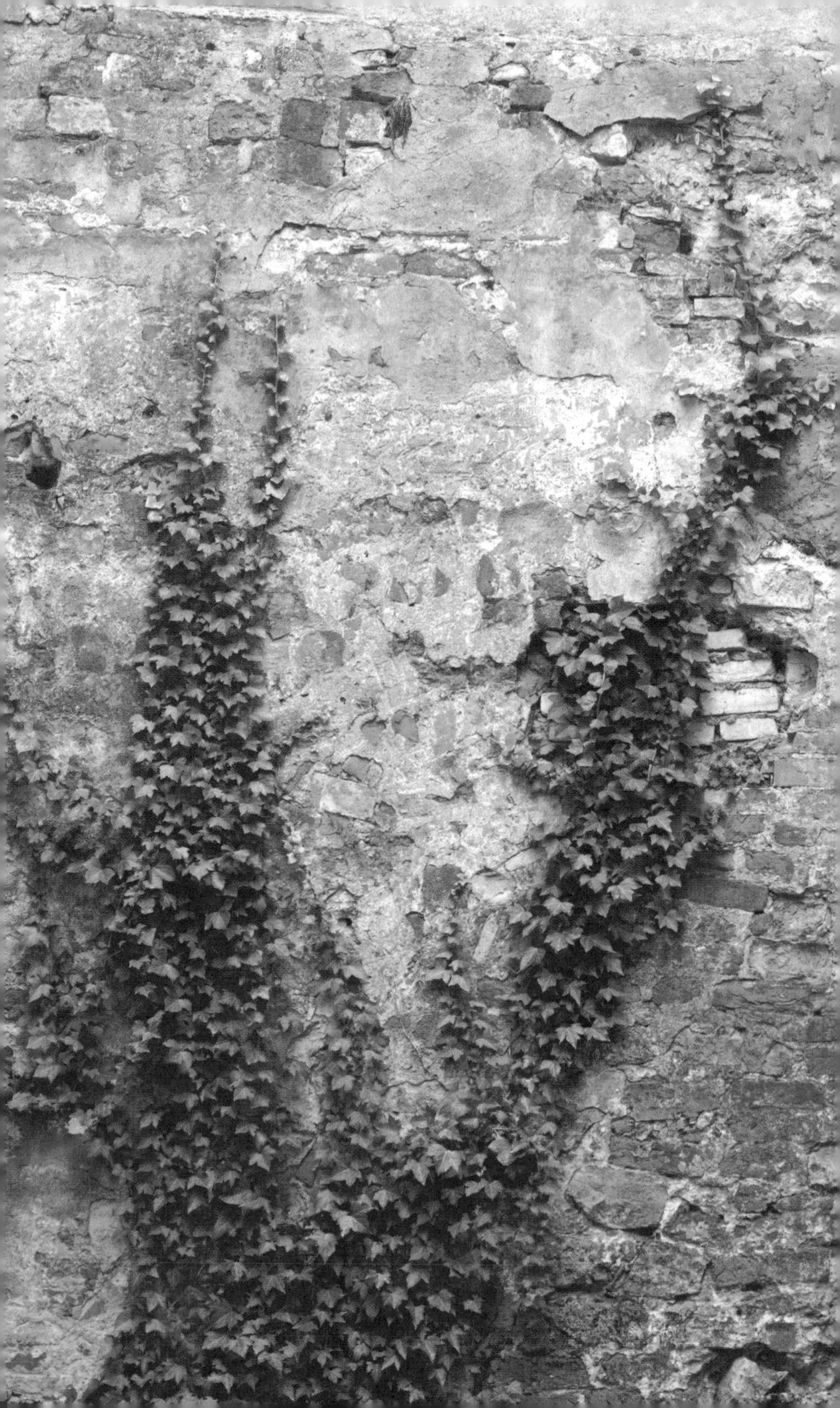

## INSPIRATION

What do you do when you aren't so sure there will be glory after you drink from a cup that seems far too bitter to survive? You remember that God has a track record of turning dark times into soil and pain into seed. This book is a testimony, not to my strength but to my broken surrender. You may be waiting on a harvest for all that you've sown, but you are God's harvest and He won't let you stay in the ground.

Friend, you are doing such important work. I want to remind you that this isn't a sprint, it's a marathon. It's not a microwave dinner, it's a slow-cooked turkey. Lasting transformation takes time, and *you are worth it*. Hang in there, sis, and keep going.

## MY PRAYER FOR YOU TODAY

———

*Father, You are wonderful. You are majestic. You are a provider. You are all-knowing. You are perfect in all Your ways. And You are a healer! Right now I entrust my sister to You. When You see her, You call her good. And I am asking You to release all of the goodness You have in store for her. Help her to see what You see in her. Lord, bless her relationships. Grant her the opportunities You've prepared for her. And open her eyes to the revelations that will unleash all You have for her. We put our trust in You in the strong name of Jesus. Amen.*

———

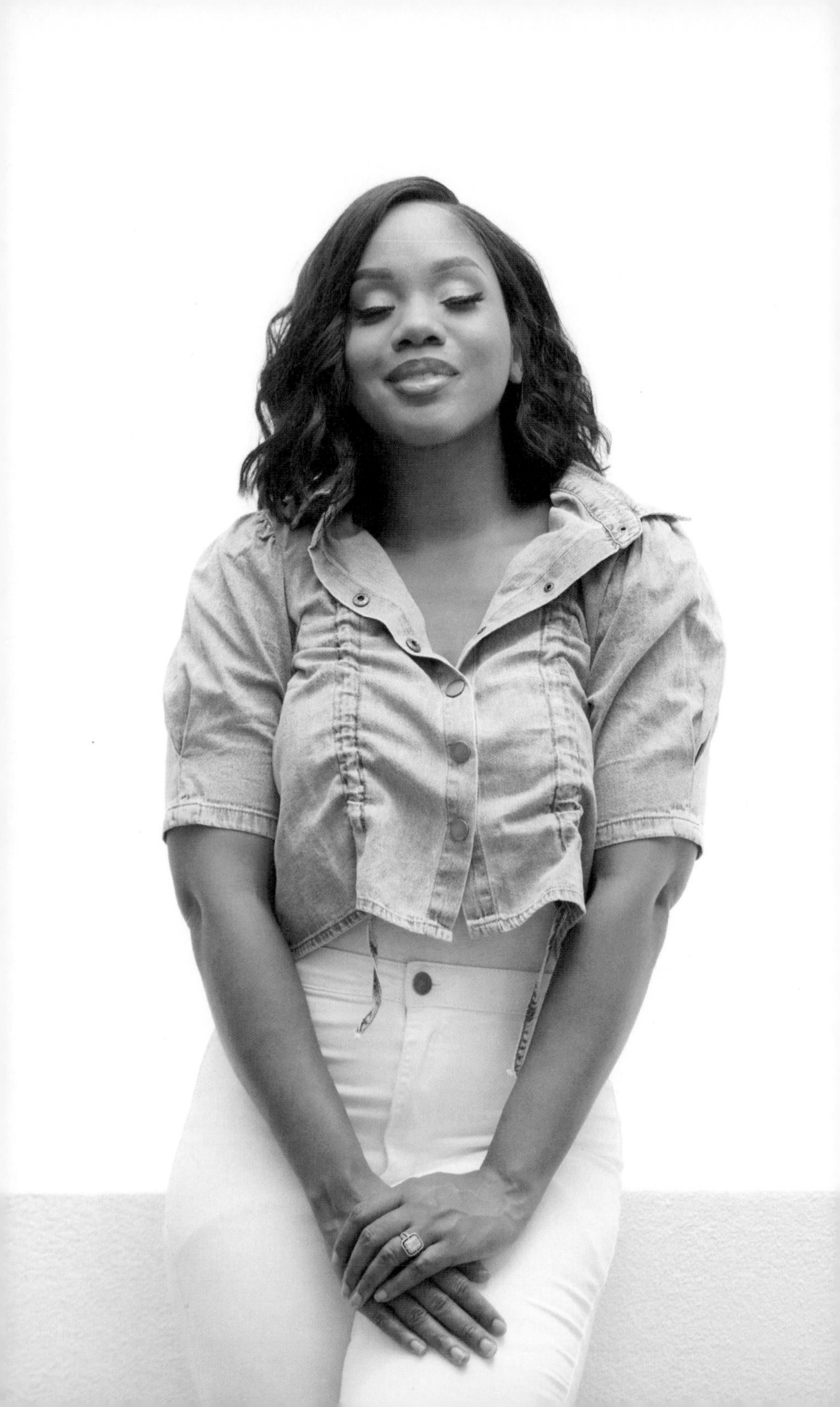

# A WAR OF SEED

*"And I will put enmity*
*Between you and the woman,*
*And between your seed and her Seed;*
*He shall bruise your head,*
*And you shall bruise His heel."*
**—GENESIS 3:15**

God has entrusted you with vision, power, talent, gifts, and anointing so you can wage war against any and every limitation this world has ever seen. What if you came to a place where you didn't just see setbacks, disappointments, and discouragement as facts of life, but rather as devils hiding in plain sight?

I'm no longer asking God to exclusively grant me wisdom, strategy, and grace for the evil I see. I'm asking God to make me aware of what is in my heart, home, or community that is at war with my ability to partner with God in bringing the world to its greatest potential. I don't know where the devils I can't see are hiding, so I have to be intentional about making sure I'm postured to defeat any negative paradigm or thought that dares to dilute the power God has given me to effect change.

It doesn't matter what seed has been fruitful in your life. Your family may have been producing the type of fruit that has caused dysfunction for generations, but it is never too late to decide that the fruit can no longer multiply with you. The moment you acknowledge that a dysfunctional seed is attempting to keep you from your divine identity, you must take action to uproot it. That act of uprooting can set you free, but it's also about much more than you. The purpose of your being delivered from your pain, shame, regret, fear, or depression is not simply for you to have a happily-ever-after. Your deliverance from everything that has so easily ensnared you is so you can become intentional about loosening the chains in another person's life.

## GOD CREATED US TO PRODUCE

The type of fruit that your family has been producing for generations does not have to be the fruit that populates your life. So I want you to consider the fruit that has come through your family line.

To the best of your ability, draw two trees. On this first tree I want you to write in the characteristics and virtues of your family that you value. *Loyalty*, *kindness*, *generosity*, *connection*, *integrity*, and *straightforwardness* are all things I'd add to my first tree.

Now, on the second tree I want you to write down the areas where bitter fruit or no fruit at all has become the norm. You have permission to be completely vulnerable and transparent about this tree. On my tree I had to acknowledge that identifying and communicating difficult emotions has not been my family's strength. The repression didn't just affect my emotions but also my spiritual development and intimacy with God.

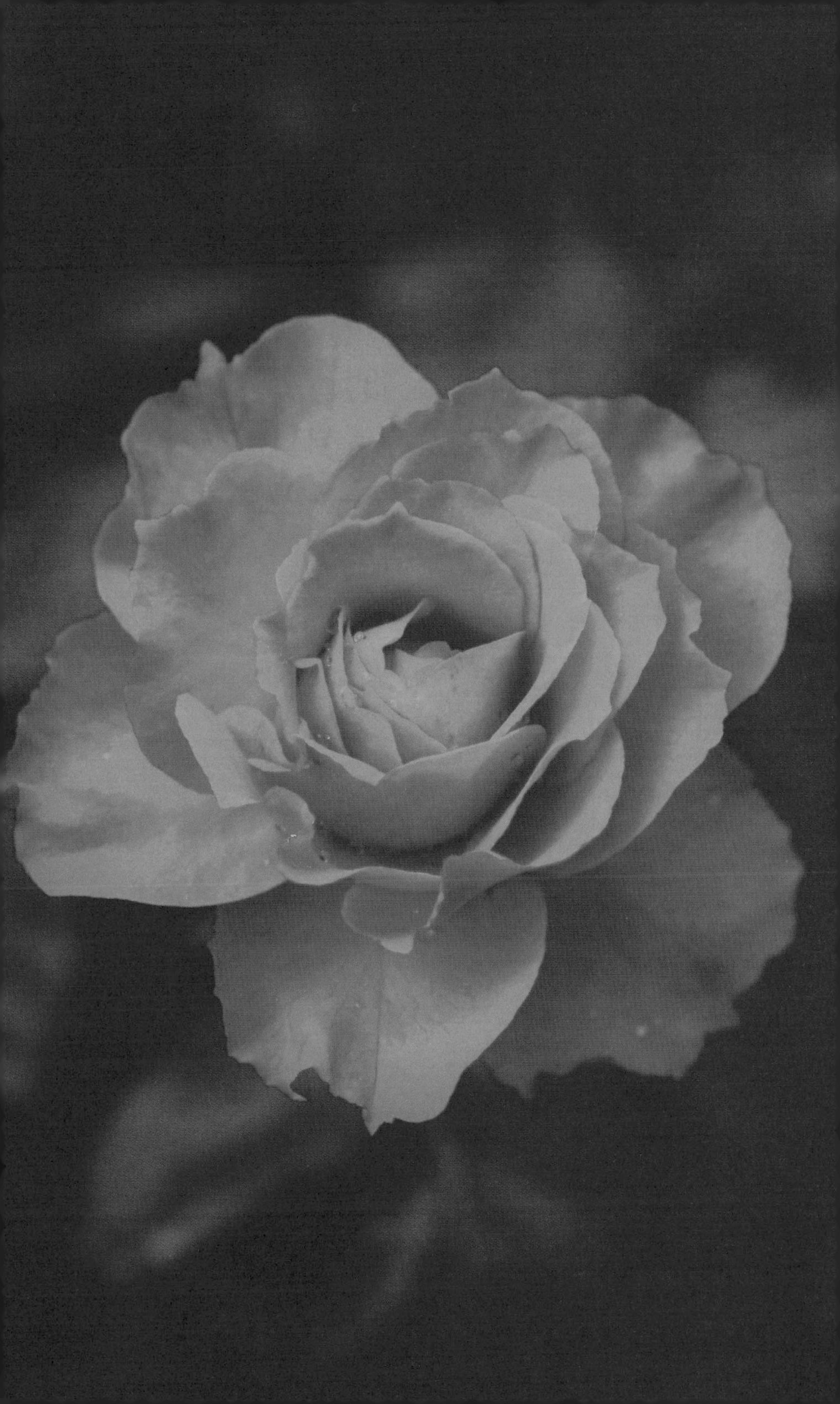

From the first tree, which characteristics do you embody today? Write them here and offer them to God.

_____

_____

_____

_____

_____

From the second tree, where are you at risk for bearing bitter fruit today? Write them here and offer them to God.

_____

_____

_____

_____

_____

## EXAMINE YOUR FRUIT

When you're aligned with who you're supposed to be in God, you have no need to hide your raw, naked vulnerability from Him. We only begin to hide when we no longer trust that we can be accepted in the truth of who we are. But God doesn't want who you can pretend to be; God wants your truth, whatever it may be!

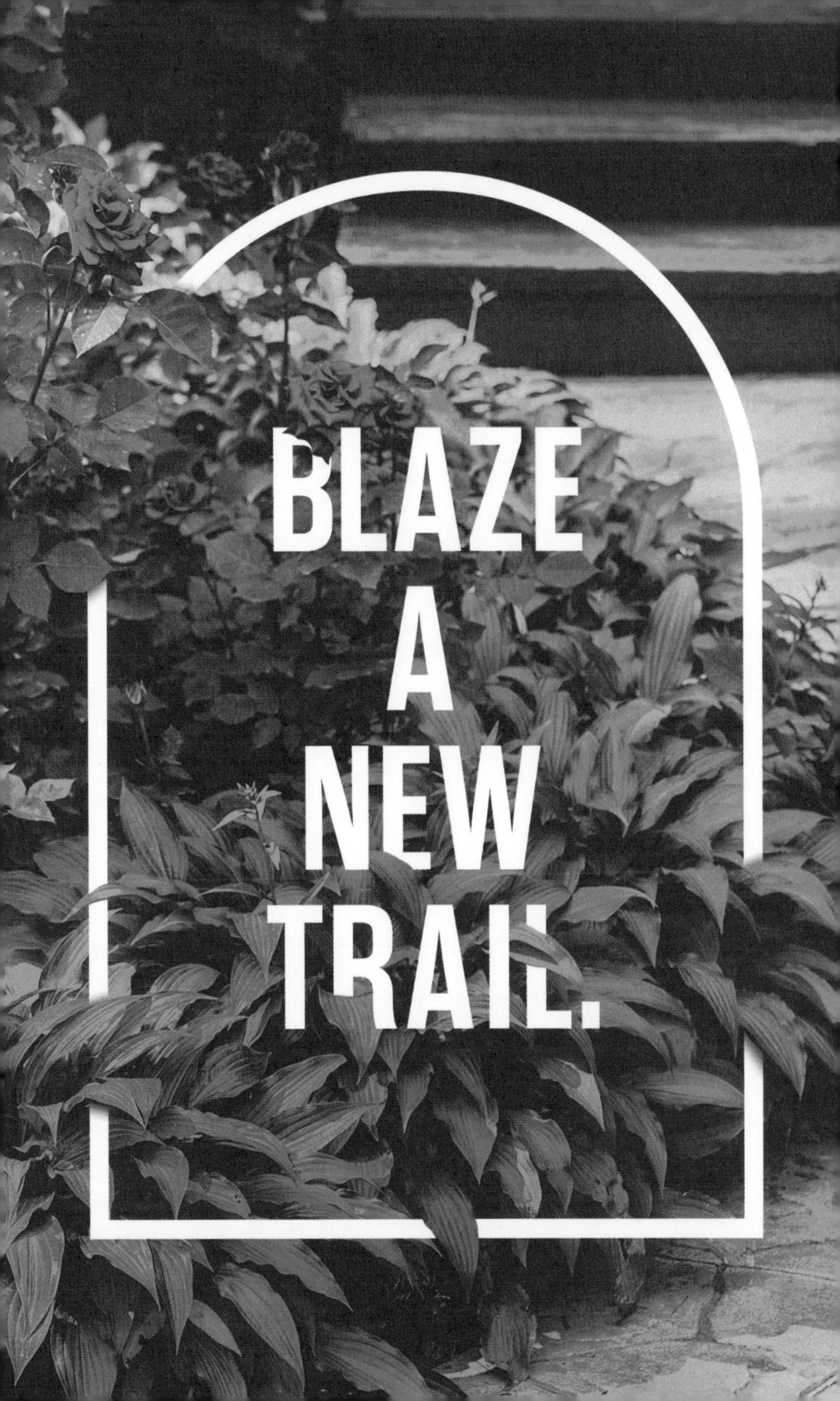
BLAZE
A
NEW
TRAIL.

## A Note from Sarah

Just because there are areas where your family may have harmful patterns, it doesn't mean that your family's worth has been diminished. And the opposite is also true. No matter how well a family has done up until now, that doesn't mean that there isn't room for even more growth. We should all desire to blaze a new trail within our families.

God wants your anger, suspicion, depression, aggression, frustration, bitterness, laziness, procrastination. Spend some time offering to God that which you'd rather hide. After you've honestly noticed and released to God that which you try to hide, quiet your heart and *listen*. What is God gently speaking to your heart?

_____

_____

_____

_____

_____

_____

## THE POWER OF THE CURSE

I've met so many women who became hostile toward themselves because of who they were or where they were in life.

Hostility is not uncommon to the woman's journey, but that hostility is not being channeled properly.

Stop being hostile to your past, body, potential, art, and creativity. Take that hostility and start using it to dismantle the narrative of shame, regret, disgust, depression, and disappointment that plagues far too many of us.

**Where are you hostile to your past? On what do you dwell?**

_____

_____

_____

_____

_____

_____

**How are you hostile to your body? How does that look?**

_____

_____

_____

_____

_____

_____

_____

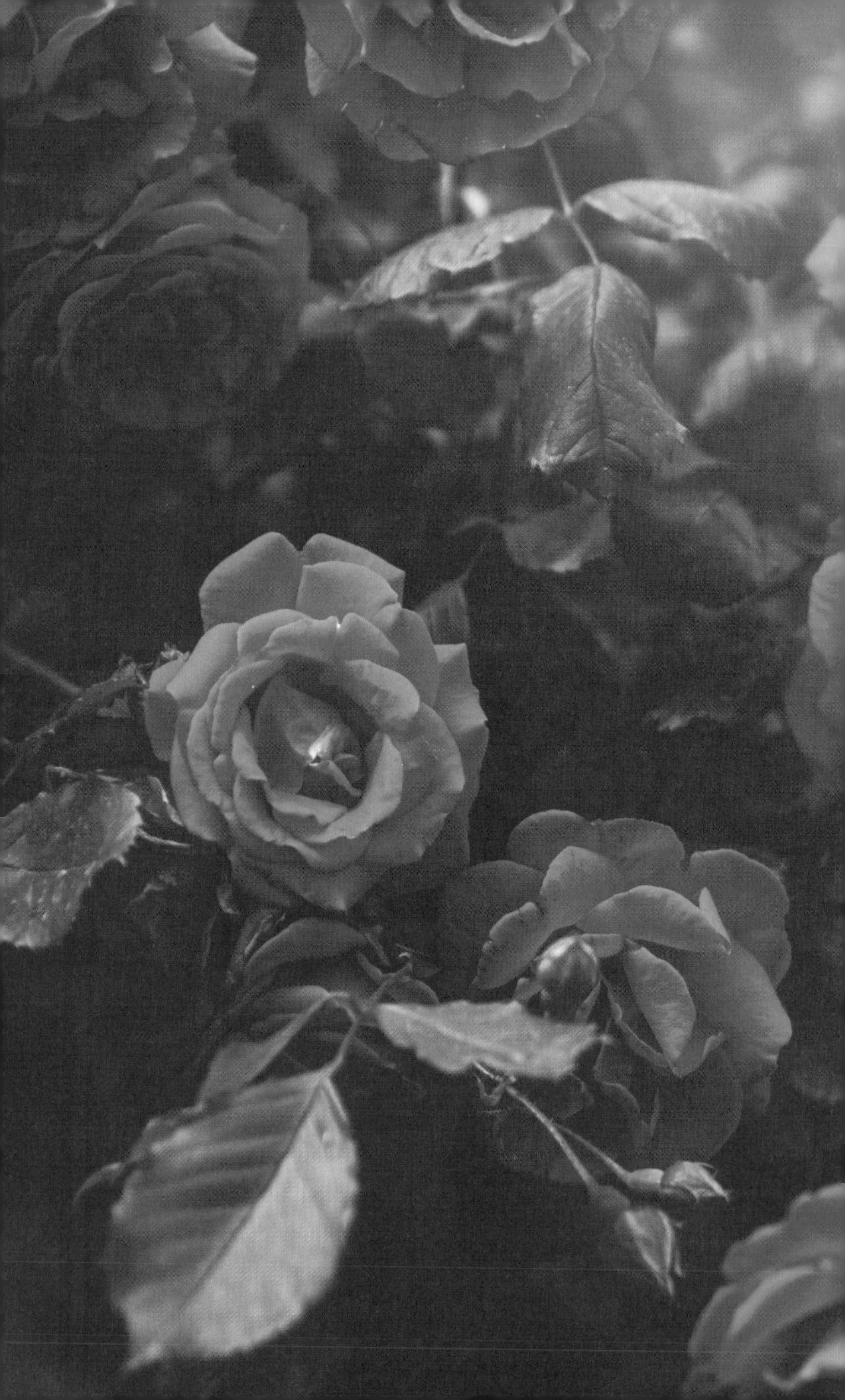

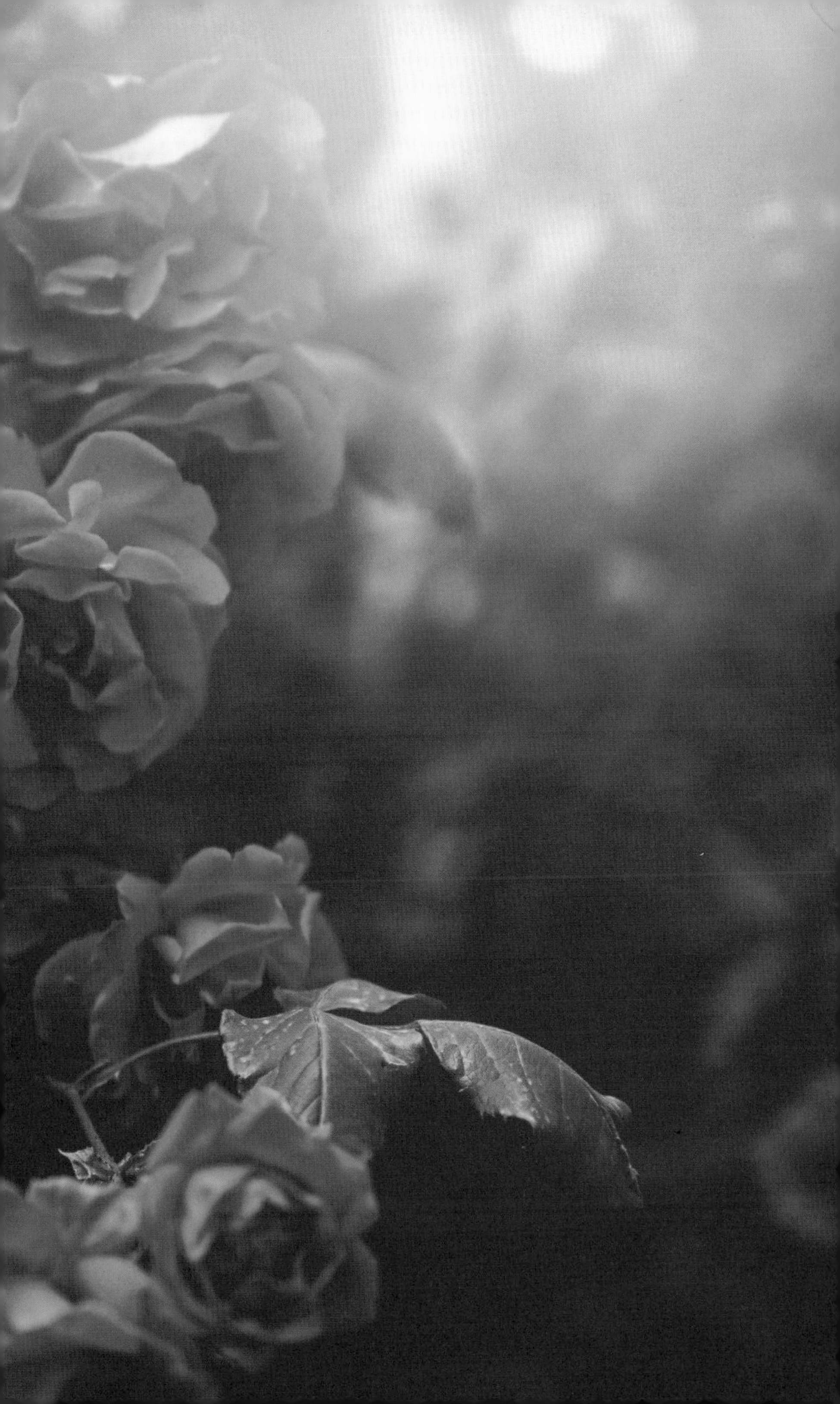

In what ways are you hostile to your potential? What potential have you not embraced?

_____

_____

_____

_____

_____

_____

Girl, I get it. I had hostility in my heart, but it was misdirected. I had hostility toward myself for being in a bad situation in the first place. I didn't know that the misplaced hostility would make me become an enemy to myself. When I finally came to the realization that I couldn't love and be hostile toward myself at the same time, I needed a place to properly direct that hostility.

What is the false narrative to which you have agreed?

_____

_____

_____

_____

_____

_____

Now flip it. What is a story—that agrees with what God says is true about you—that is truer than the one you've believed?

_____

_____

_____

_____

_____

## ACCESS GOD'S HELP

In the garden of Eden all the Serpent had was seed. That seed took root in Eve's life. It changed the way she thought, and then it changed the way she acted. That's why we can leave no room for even the smallest seed of division, confusion, disappointment, or depression.

## HOW TO PRAY

The moment we acknowledge that a seed has been planted that is trying to strip us of our identity, we must take action to uproot it.

Close your eyes and ask God to show you any seed that's been planted in you that seeks to strip you of your identity.

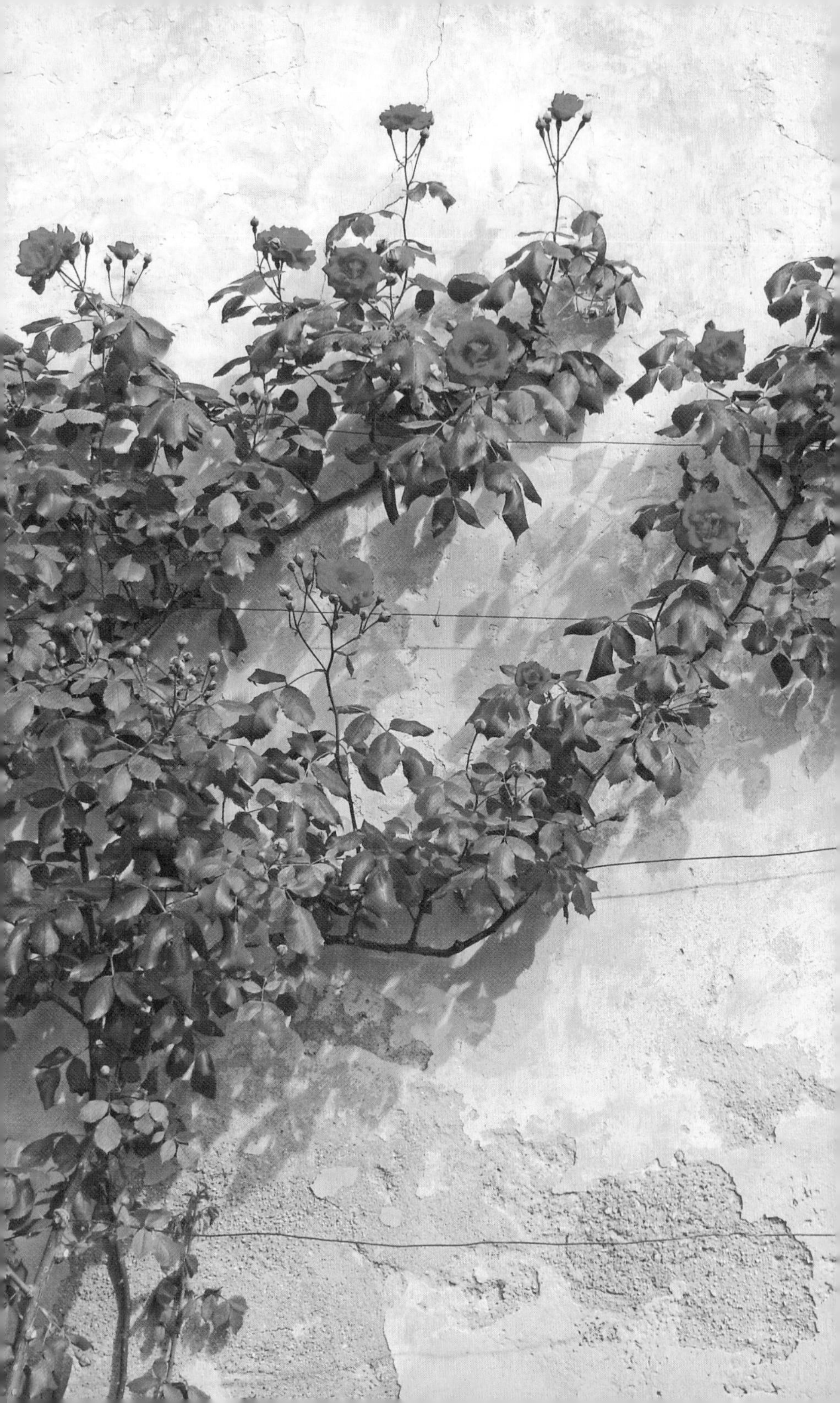

When God shows you that seed, ask Him what your next step should be. What is *one action* that you can take to uproot it?

_____

_____

_____

_____

_____

We must also recognize that God desires to give us seed. God wants to give us seed that will help us defeat whatever stands in our way.

Close your eyes and ask God to show you what seed He's planted in you that will help you defeat anything that stands in your way.

When God shows you that seed, ask Him what your next step should be. What is *one action* that you can take to move forward?

_____

_____

_____

_____

_____

# INSPIRATION

God wants you to know that what you call *emptiness*, He calls *soil*. Just as God did in Genesis, when He directed the earth to bring forth fruit and it did, when His will aligns with your hunger, you will bring forth every seed God has placed in you. Seed is so much bigger than a gift or talent, though it can be that. The seed that God gives you is the part of your identity that looks like God. Maintaining kindness in a cruel world is seed. Being faithful over a craft that infiltrates and changes hearts for the better is seed. Serving is seed. Patience is seed. When the fruit of God's Spirit shows up in your life, that is God's seed in you combating the Serpent's seed.

# MY PRAYER FOR YOU TODAY

*Giver of life and Sower of seed, I believe You created my sister to bear good fruit. As she comes vulnerably before You, open her eyes to any bitter fruit You want to uproot from her heart, and by Your power defeat the Serpent's seed. Show her the good fruit she is producing—in her life and in the lives of others—and nourish her to continue bearing that which You have planted in her. By Your mighty power, bring forth every seed You have placed in her, for Your glory. Amen.*

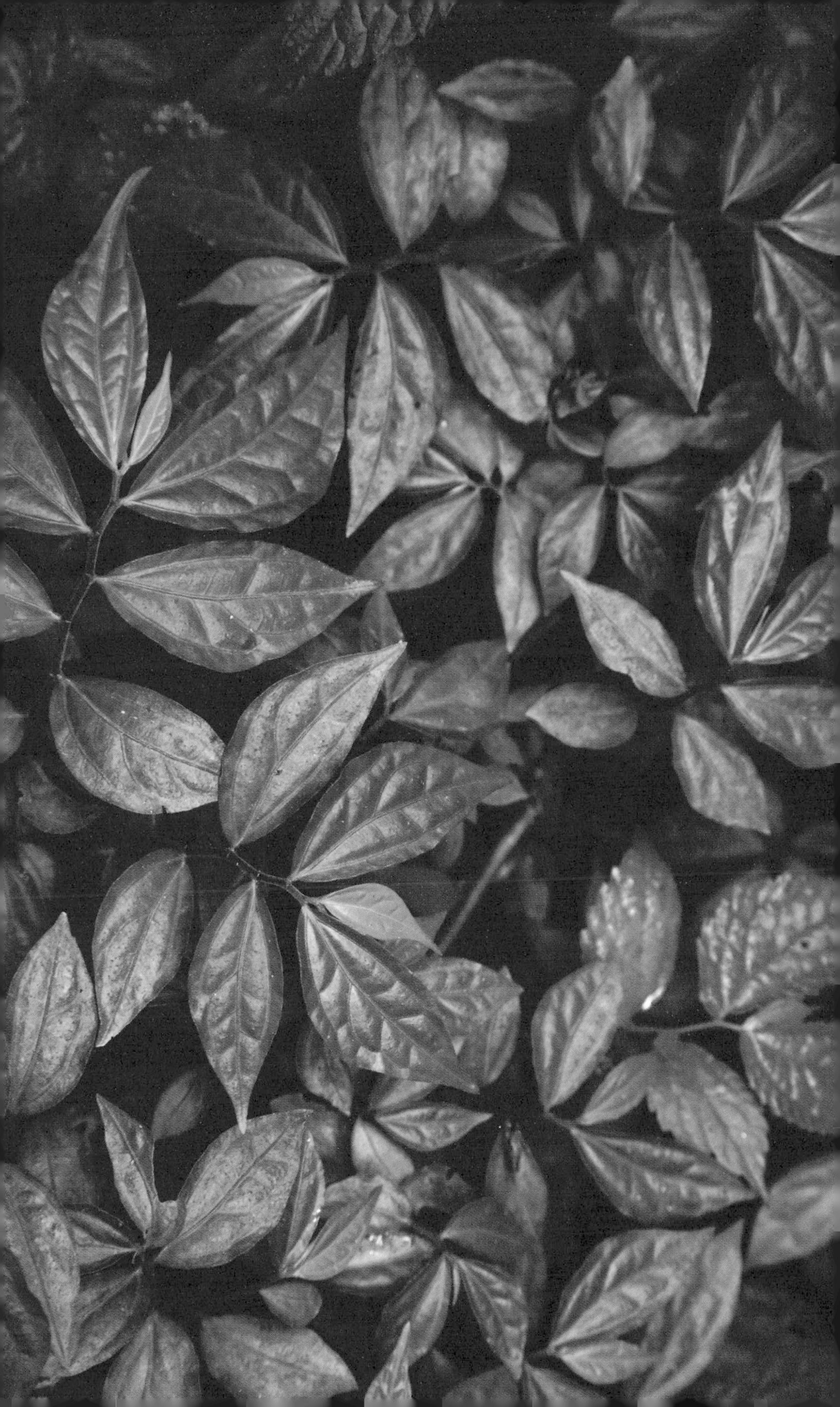

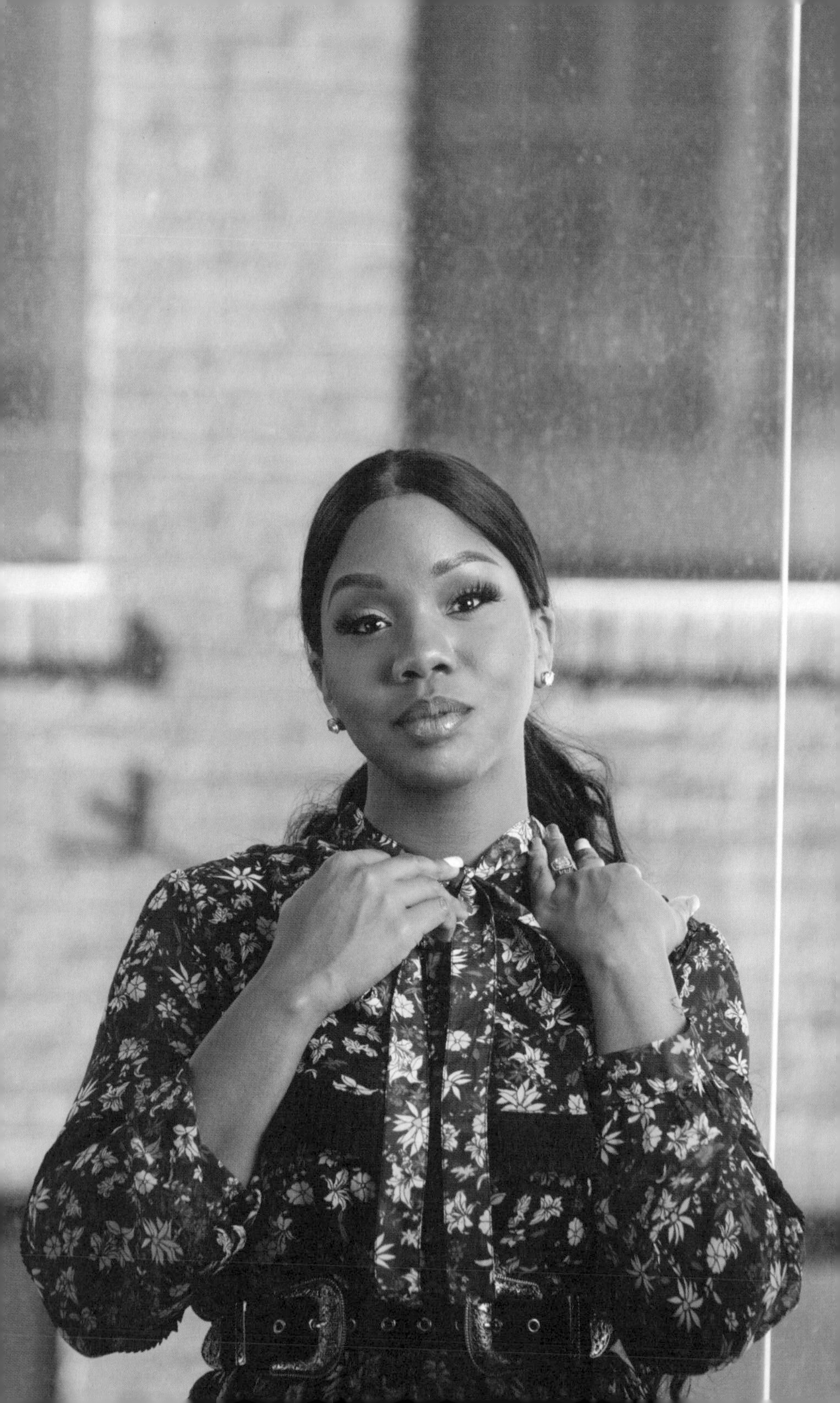

# CHAPTER FIVE

# WORK THE WAIT

*And Adam called his wife's name Eve, because she was the mother of all living.*

—GENESIS 3:20

As we begin to do the inner work that leads us closer and closer to God's perfect plan for our lives, we can expect to discover purpose and passion that makes us ponder, *Maybe this is why I was born.*

Generally, when we think about who we are, we begin by naming off the titles and roles we possess. I am a wife, mother, daughter, entrepreneur, leader, pastor, and author. Actually, that's not who I am; it's what I do. But it can be exceptionally hard to know the difference.

Answering the question of who you are is impossible without understanding your essence. Ask yourself, *What is my consistent offering to my job, family, friends, and community?*

I am a servant, lover, carrier of joy, motivator, facilitator of environments, listener, and believer. Those qualities make up who I am, but they also show up in each of my roles. And the combination of those qualities gives me distinction regardless of the environment I'm in.

While we do not want to make the mistake of making who we are become synonymous with what we do, we can't ignore what we do altogether. What we do and how we do it should all stem from who we are.

My servanthood, love, joy, listening, believing, and facilitation of environments all show up in how I function as a wife, mother, daughter, entrepreneur, leader, pastor, and author. And the qualities and gifts you bring to the world show up in your roles as well.

*Warm Up:* If someone had asked your ten-year-old girl self what you'd be or do when you were an adult, what would you have answered? What would have been the big dream in your heart?

_____

_____

_____

_____

_____

_____

_____

## MAYBE THIS IS WHY I WAS BORN

Just like me, your qualities and gifts are expressed in your various roles. To get at those qualities and gifts you've been given to share with the world God loves, ask yourself, *What is my consistent offering to my job, family, friends, and community?* Take some time with this and reflect on the offerings you share.

_____

_____

_____

_____

## PURPOSE HAPPENS IN STEPS

Right now you're a seed who's learning the beauty of being planted, nurtured, and nourished so you can provide sustenance to the world. So let's slow down and notice what God is up to in you right now.

*Agree.* You must come into agreement that your existence is seed. Stop to acknowledge that you're here to become more and more like what God had in mind. Here you can write a sentence of agreement, letting God know you're on board:

_____

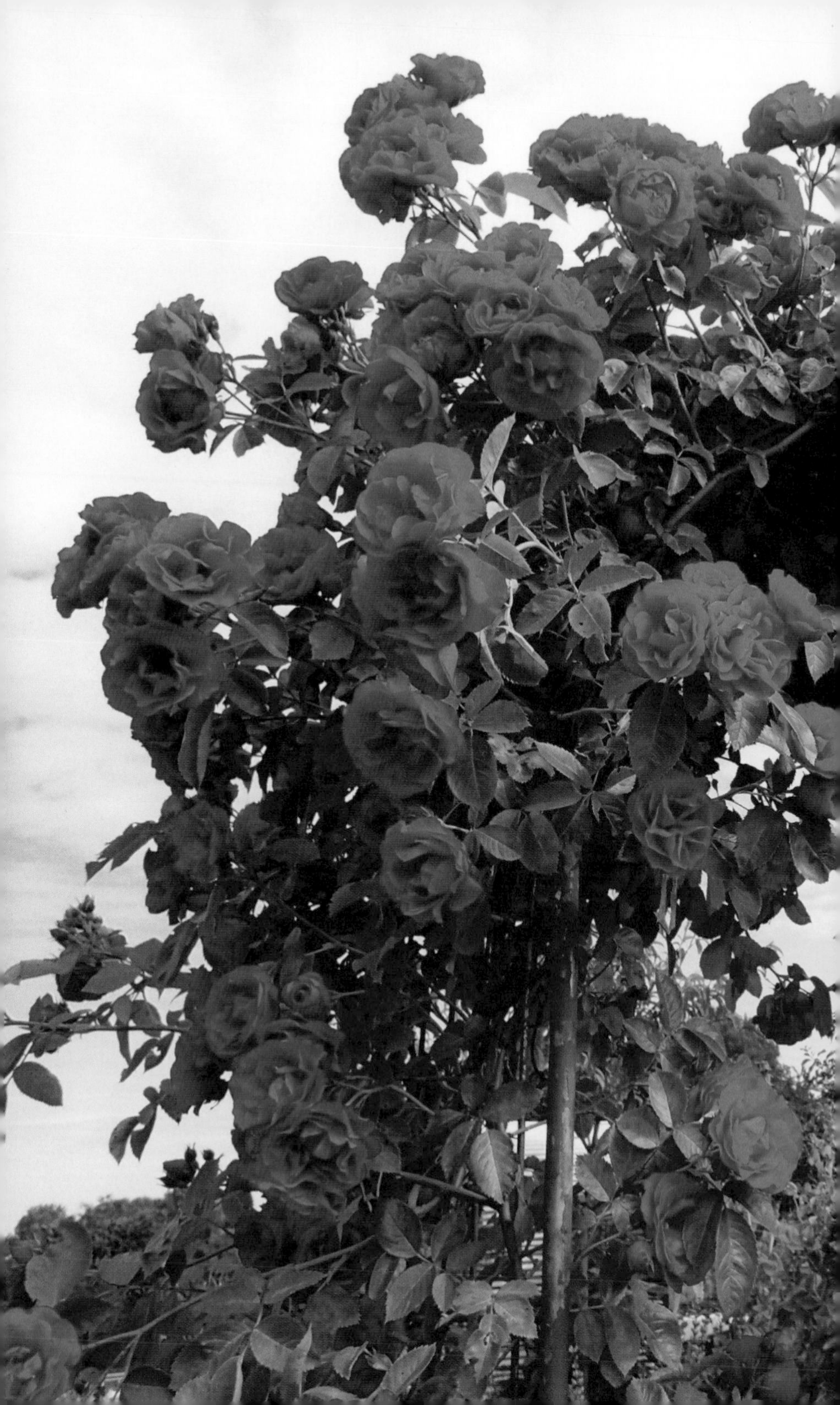

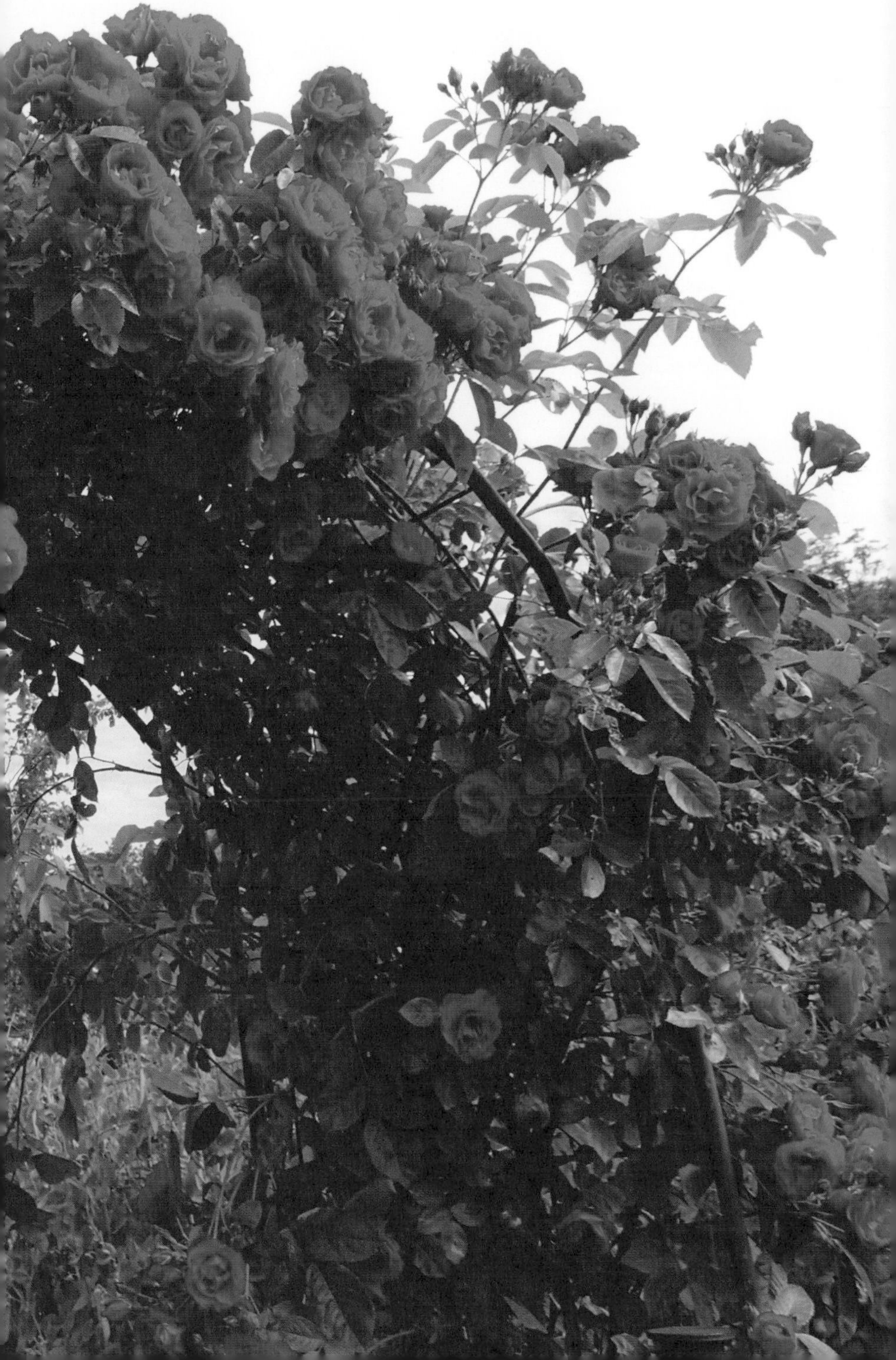

_____

_____

_____

_____

_____

*Protect.* Because you aren't exactly sure who you are becoming, you must make sure to protect your environment from any habit, friendship, relationship, or opportunity that could stunt your growth.

What elements in your environment can stunt what God wants to do in you and through you?

_____

_____

_____

_____

_____

You need people and opportunities in your life that reflect who you're becoming. List some of those people and opportunities.

_____

_____

_____

_____

_____

*Nurture.* Finally, when your fruit seed begins to take root, you have to consider how you can continue the act of nurturing it. You will know that something is nurturing your seed when it begins to cut through your fears and insecurities and begins to motivate and empower you. This may come from reading a book like you're doing now, hearing a speech, listening to a song, or connecting with someone you know.

Note those recent moments when you—or someone else!— have nourished your seed:

_____

_____

_____

_____

_____

## NOTICE THE CLUES!

God gave Eve a word about the role she was to play in helping God establish presence in the earth. Instead of asking God to

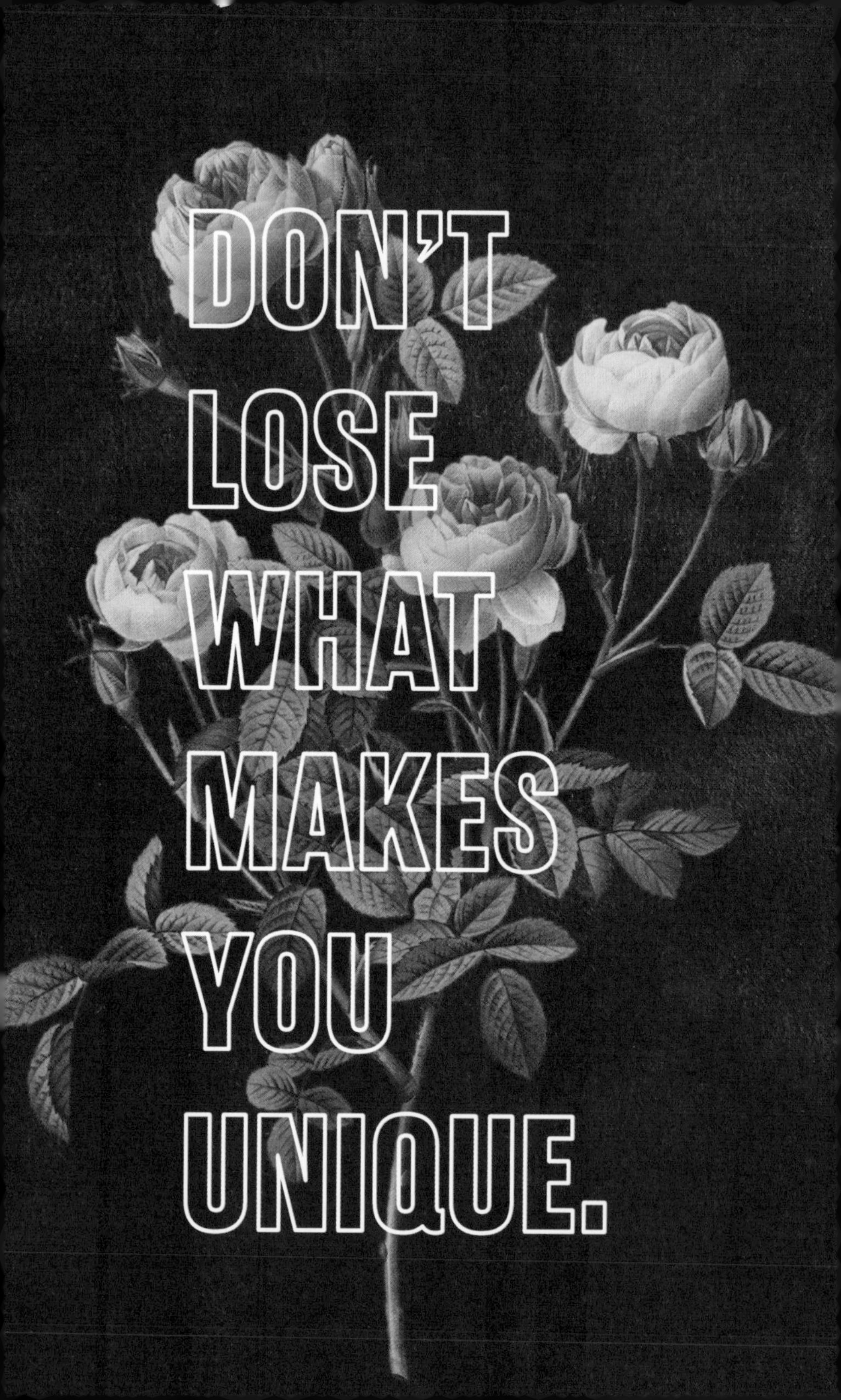
DON'T
LOSE
WHAT
MAKES
YOU
UNIQUE.

tell you your purpose, try asking God what role you can play in establishing His presence on the earth. *Purpose* is an individual assignment reserved for each person to work in tandem with God to bring heaven to earth.

Where are you most passionate about seeing the character of God show up in the earth? Is it for teen moms, the criminal justice system, foster care, church, entertainment? That passion is trying to give you a clue about where you can partner with God.

Think back on the moments and seasons—throughout your lifetime—when you felt in sync with God in bringing heaven to earth. In what arenas, and among what people, did you find joy in serving? (Be thorough! Start in your childhood and prayerfully notice the spots when you had a distinct sense of living out your purpose.)

_____

_____

_____

_____

_____

_____

_____

_____

Today, where are you most passionate about seeing the character of God show up in the earth? What industry or people do you feel God is calling you to?

_____

_____

_____

_____

_____

## YOUR OPPORTUNITY TO DREAM

Imagine yourself at the height of success. Don't be limited by certain industries, qualifications, or experience. This is your opportunity to dream. Running a fashion house? Heading up a Fortune 500 company? Teaching at a school that considers a student's total well-being? Whatever it is, jot it down.

_____

_____

_____

_____

_____

Then think through these two questions.

What are the most important character traits you must possess to maximize your dream role?

- 
- 
- 
- 
- 

How are those skills showing up where you are now?

_____

_____

_____

_____

_____

## ACCESS GOD'S HELP

When you were ten, there was an adult version of you that you'd imagined: Ballerina. Doctor. Professional roller skater. And *today* there's that little seed of a dream in your heart of who you might evolve to become. It's important to stay open to what God might have for you while you seek God's perfect plan.

## A Note from Sarah

It's naive to think the traits and skills you'll need will emerge overnight. They are muscles that must be exercised in your now so they can be strong for your future.

Invite God to guide you. Ask God to help you release what you no longer need and to see the vision *He has* for your life today.

- Father God, show me the *old* version of me that You are inviting me to release.
- Help me to see the ones I am called to serve and bless.
- Show me what skills and gifts I can hone to best serve You.

Now write your prayer to God here:

Dear God,

_____

_____

_____

_____

_____

_____

_____

_____

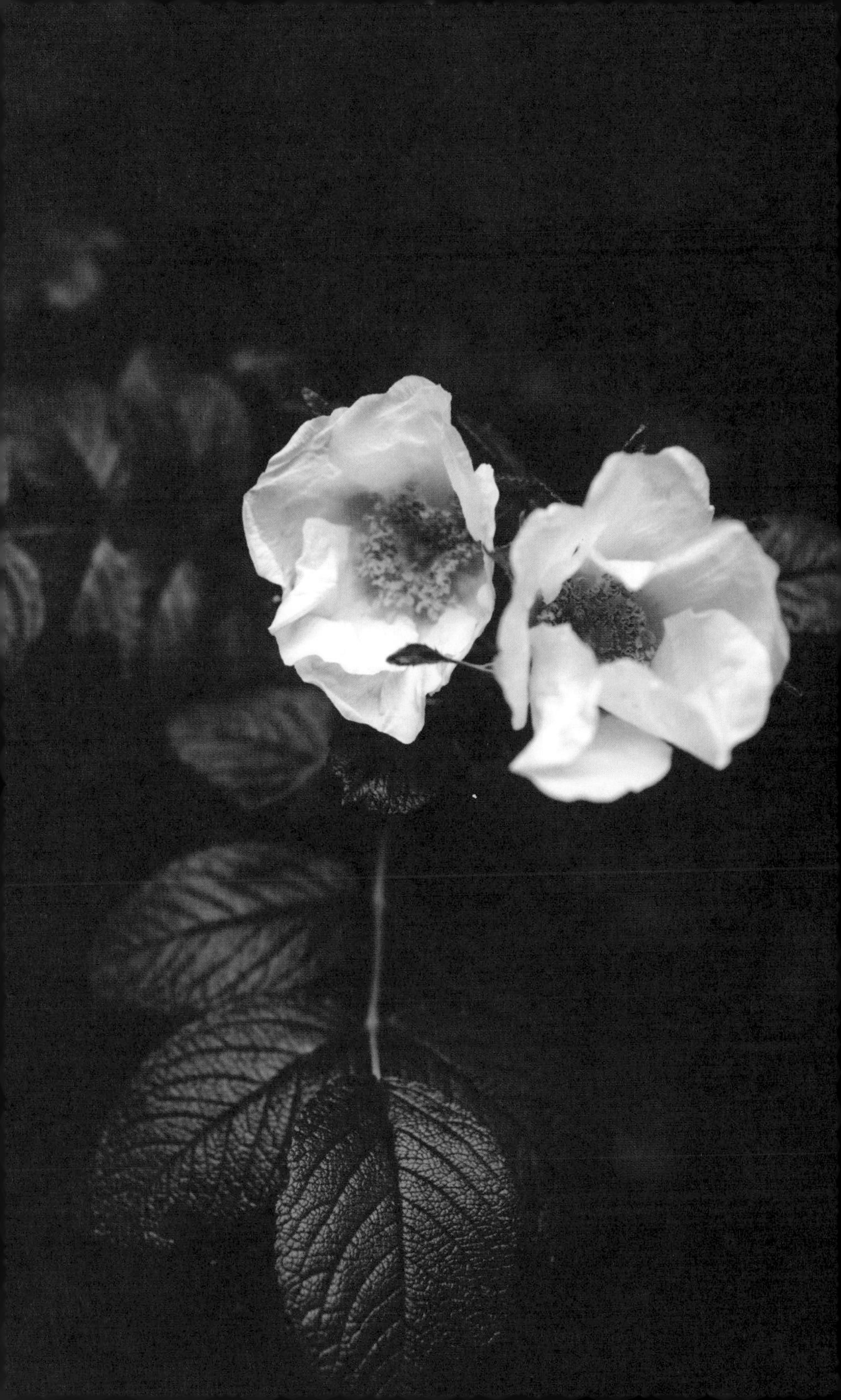

## INSPIRATION

Where you are right now may not be connected to where you will land, but where you are right now will serve you when you get to where you're headed. So while you're exercising the muscles you'll need for the journey ahead of you, make sure you don't lose what makes you unique.

When God gives you an opportunity, He isn't expecting you to become someone else to fulfill it. He created that opportunity for a specific, authentic version of you. The counterfeit version of you may squeeze into that space, but eventually you will have to choose to be who you truly are or risk not being able to experience the fullness of why God has placed an opportunity in your path.

Everyone has tried to force a puzzle piece to fit in a space that it's not made for. You cram it in there and try to ignore the fact that your thumb almost went numb trying to smash it in. You're so ready to move on to the next part of the puzzle that you don't think that one little piece will matter. Then what happens? You can't even enjoy the rest of the puzzle because you see that one little piece bulging out from what was supposed to be a beautiful picture.

On this journey, commit to being the most authentic version of yourself.

# MY PRAYER FOR YOU TODAY

---

*God, I thank You that my sister is evolving to become the woman You created her to be. As she comes vulnerably before You, show her what You see! As she faithfully seeks the purpose You have for her, open her eyes to anything that could hinder what You have for her. And show her the seeds You've already planted within her that she is being called to honor and nourish. We put our trust in You, as the One who makes all things grow. Amen.*

---

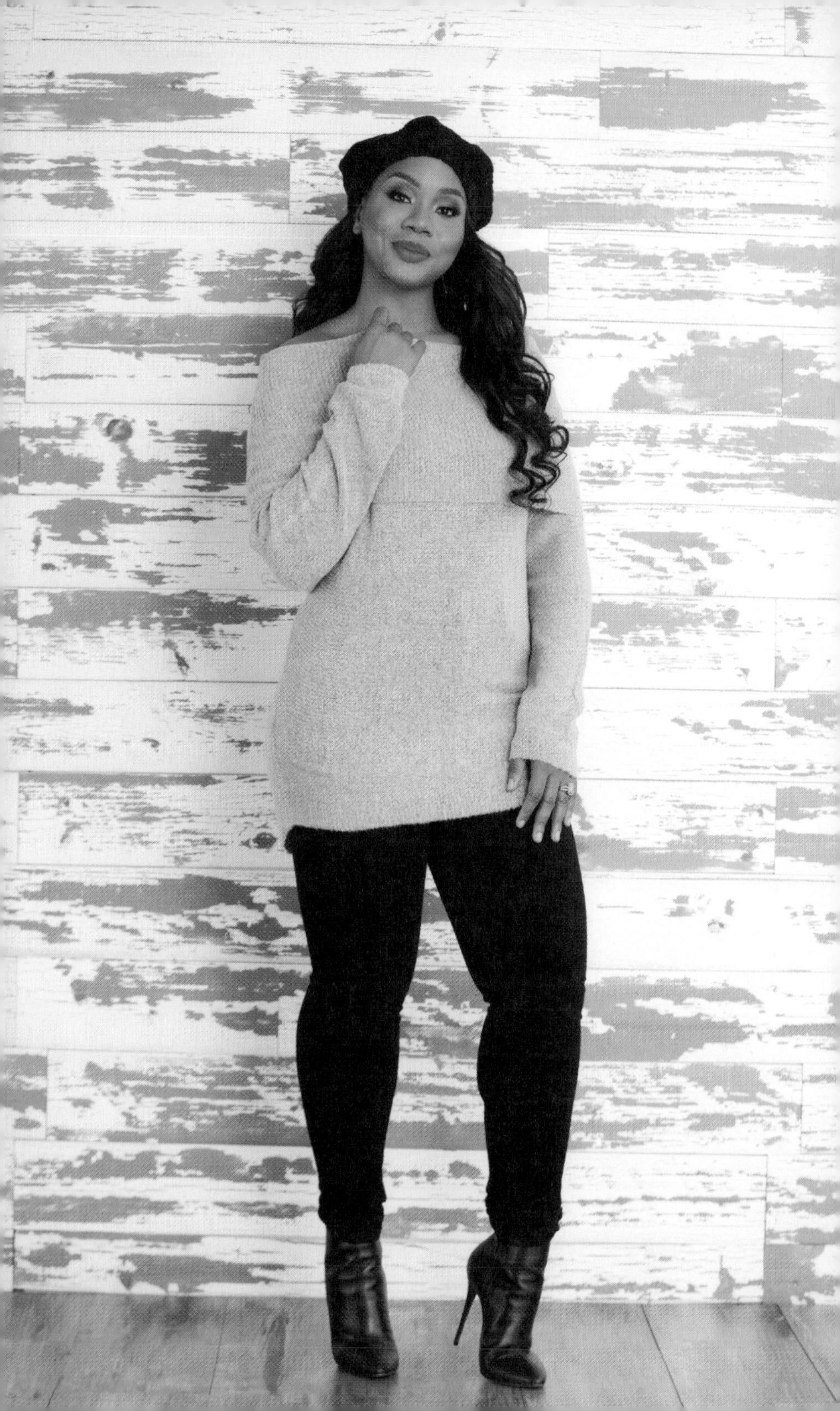

# CHAPTER SIX

# IT'LL NEVER ADD UP

*Then Jesus lifted up His eyes, and seeing a great multitude coming toward Him, He said to Philip, "Where shall we buy bread, that these may eat?" But this He said to test him, for He Himself knew what He would do.*

—JOHN 6:5–6

After Jesus preached and healed people, a crowd of people began to follow Him. "Where shall we buy bread, that these may eat?" Jesus asked the disciples.

Andrew responded, "There is a lad here who has five barley loaves and two small fish, but what are they among so many?" (John 6:9).

The food donated from a young boy in the crowd certainly

wasn't enough to feed five-thousand-plus people. What was Jesus thinking?

Only a child would turn over the little he had to a stranger who was trying to feed that many people. I can tell you right now that as an adult I would have had some questions. I would have tried to be polite and suppress my discomfort, but I don't just let people walk away with food I'm planning to eat. At least not without some serious interrogation. Girl, if my husband took my dinner plate away from me at the house, I would probably hit the roof, so a stranger would not stand a chance. This boy represents a beautiful vulnerability that I'm challenged to strive for each and every day. I admire how he was able to offer and trust what little he had to another person.

Jesus multiplied what the boy offered, and I'm convinced that Jesus multiplies your offering as well.

## WHEN IT FEELS TOO BIG

There's no way that boy could've known that the small lunch he possessed could be used to bless a multitude. Jesus' mission was not only to redeem humanity but also to raise up individuals who could continue to spread awareness of humanity's ability to rise above fear, anxiety, insecurity, shame, pride, ego, and all the other bitter fruit that the Serpent planted in the garden.

Has there ever been a moment in your life when you were placed in a position to do something that seemed bigger than you, and you decided to shrink back to what you know?

_____

_____

_____

_____

_____

Has there ever been a moment in your life when you were placed in a position to do something that seemed bigger than you, and you trusted that you could learn as you went?

_____

_____

_____

_____

_____

Note: If we walk away from what God tells us to do, then we won't find peace anywhere else. What that means, sis, is that now is the time to put on your big-girl panties and figure out

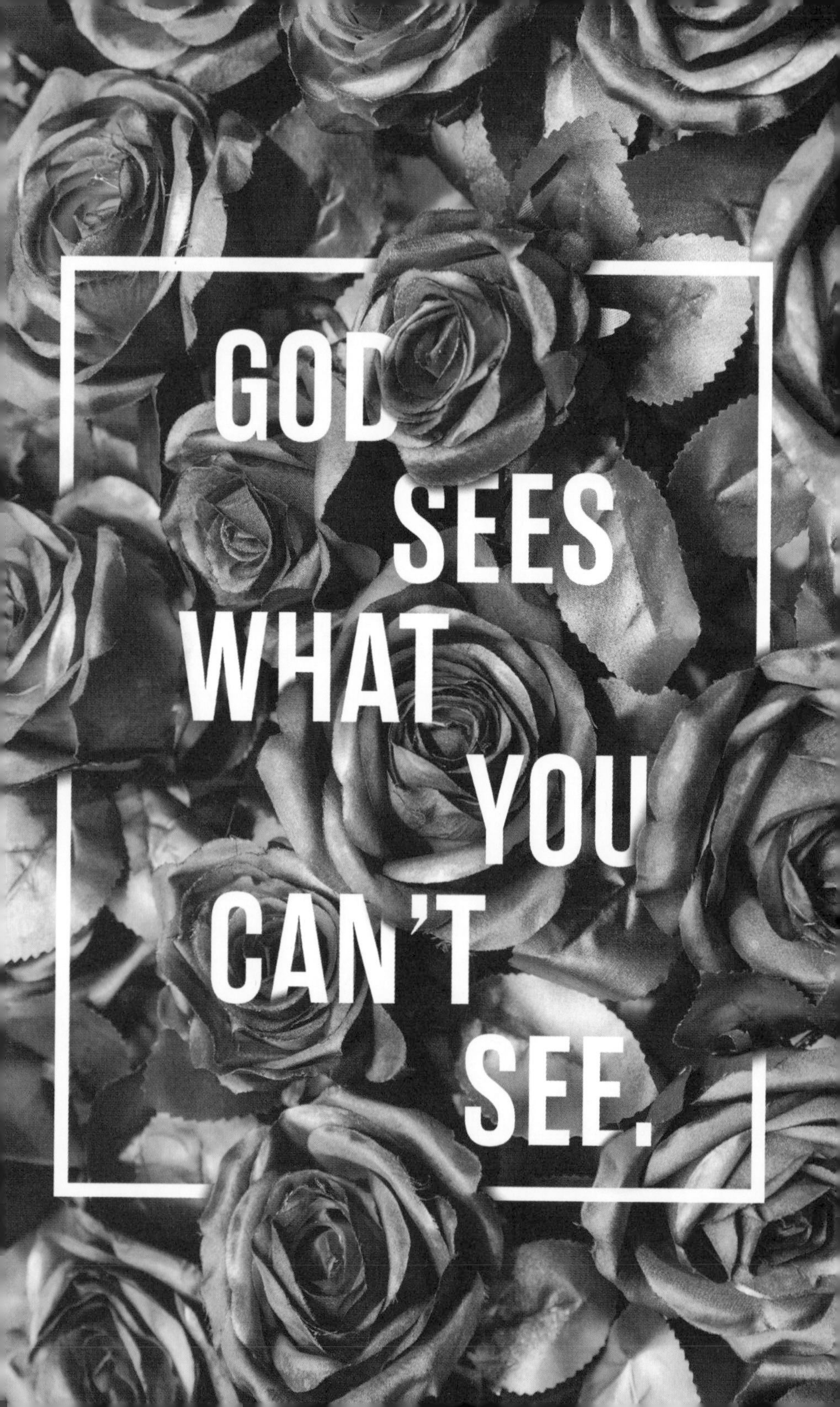
GOD SEES WHAT YOU CAN'T SEE.

how to overcome the obstacle that's in your way. (But only if you want to live with peace.)

## FEELING NOT ENOUGH

When your faith brings you into a situation that feels greater than you, it can be overwhelming. When you feel like there's a possibility you are not educated, experienced, connected, exposed, or polished enough, you must recognize that all those moments come down to not feeling like you have the proper resources.

Gaining wisdom and education so you can become well-versed for your present circumstance does not mean you are no longer being authentic. Being authentic doesn't mean you'll never grow and change. Authenticity is taking what you've learned and applying it in a way that is unique to how you process, communicate, and create.

My grandmother always said, "Life is a classroom, and we're all students." In other words, we are constantly learning and harnessing what we've learned for the road ahead of us. The goal is to be true to who you are and where you are.

**Where do you feel under-resourced?**

_____

_____

_____

_____

_____

Instead of using blanket thoughts and statements like "I don't have what it takes," try to get specific about where and what you lack for a specific task. For instance, in a corporate setting you may feel like you're not qualified for the role or promotion that you'd like. As a student, you may feel like you don't have the resources to dedicate the time you need to your studies. Mothers may feel ill-equipped to raise emotionally healthy children.

What is it you need that you feel you are lacking today?

_____

_____

_____

_____

_____

Once you've identified the area where you feel like you don't have what it takes, consider what the outcome would be if you were sufficiently resourced.

_____

_____

_____

_____

_____

I believe the most admirable thing the disciples did after taking into consideration how to feed the hungry multitude was that they then began looking for unconventional methods of accomplishing their goal. The disciples could have been married to the notion that the only way to feed the multitude was to send them back to town. But had they been married to that formula, they would have missed Jesus' miracle.

Think beyond the way things have "always been done." What is another way to do what God is calling you to do? (Take your time. Listen for God's leading.)

_____

_____

_____

_____

_____

## ACCESSING WHAT YOU CAN

You have to be willing to ask God if there's something already available that could assist you in becoming better prepared.

Take inventory of what you do have instead of lamenting over what you don't have.

- *Borrow other people's knowledge.* You may not have the background for the present you're standing in, but someone does.

What relationships with people ahead of you on the path can you seek out? (Don't be afraid to ask them, but be intentional about what you want to learn from them.)

_____

_____

_____

_____

_____

You don't even have to know a person to borrow their knowledge. What books, interviews, podcasts, or social media can you access to borrow the knowledge of others?

- 

- 

- 

- 

-

*Be unconventional.* Okay, so I didn't finish college. But when I wanted to know about business, I started looking up the textbooks for business management classes, ordered them online, and began teaching myself principles in business management.

Is there an unconventional strategy you can utilize that will prepare you to take your next step?

- 
- 
- 
- 
- 

*Ask questions.* Ask your questions. In honor of great teachers everywhere, make a point to remember one of my educator's favorite sayings: "There's no such thing as a stupid question."

Begin to make a list here of the questions to which you need answers. (Also implement a system on your phone or computer where you can keep track of these questions and their answers!)

- 
- 
-

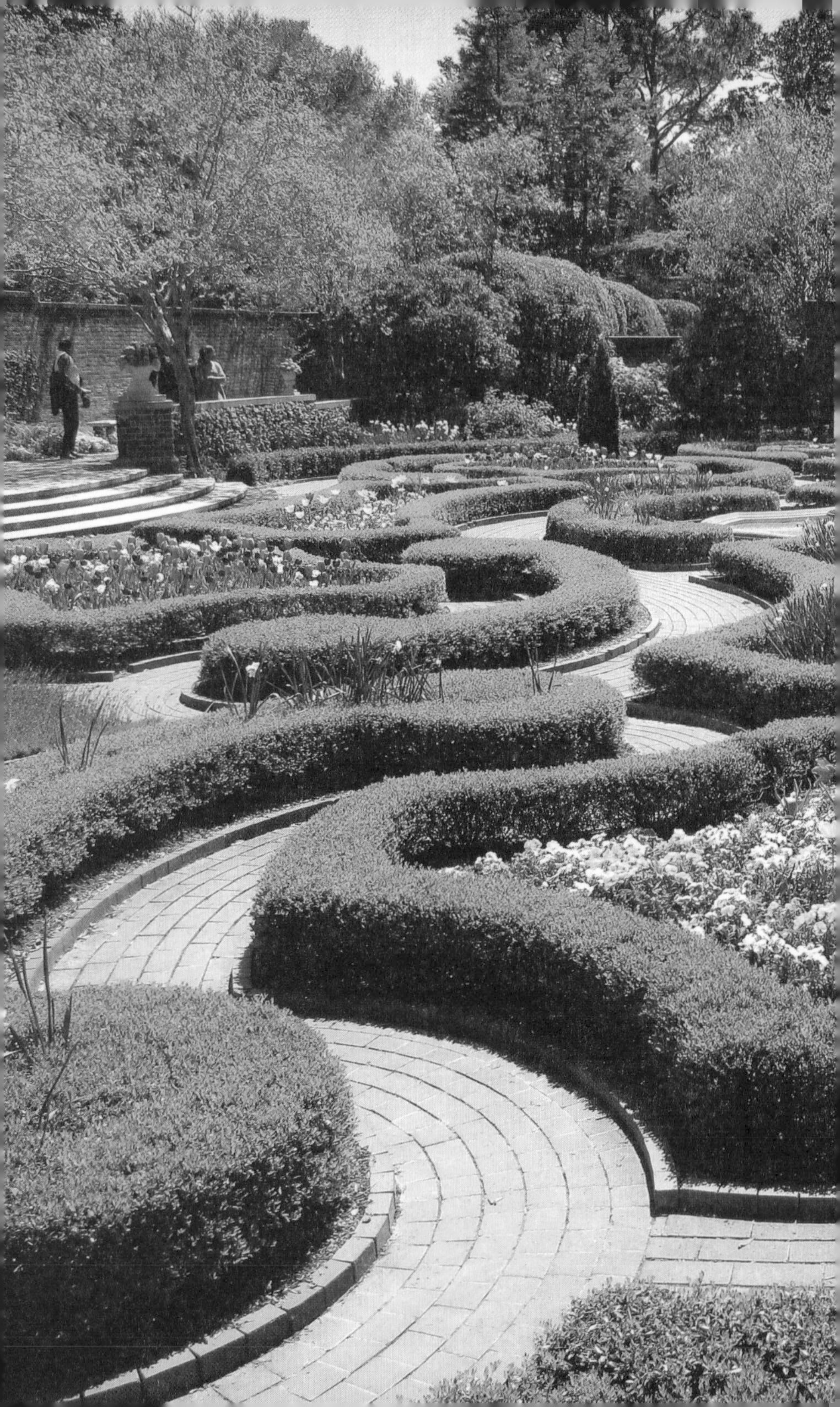

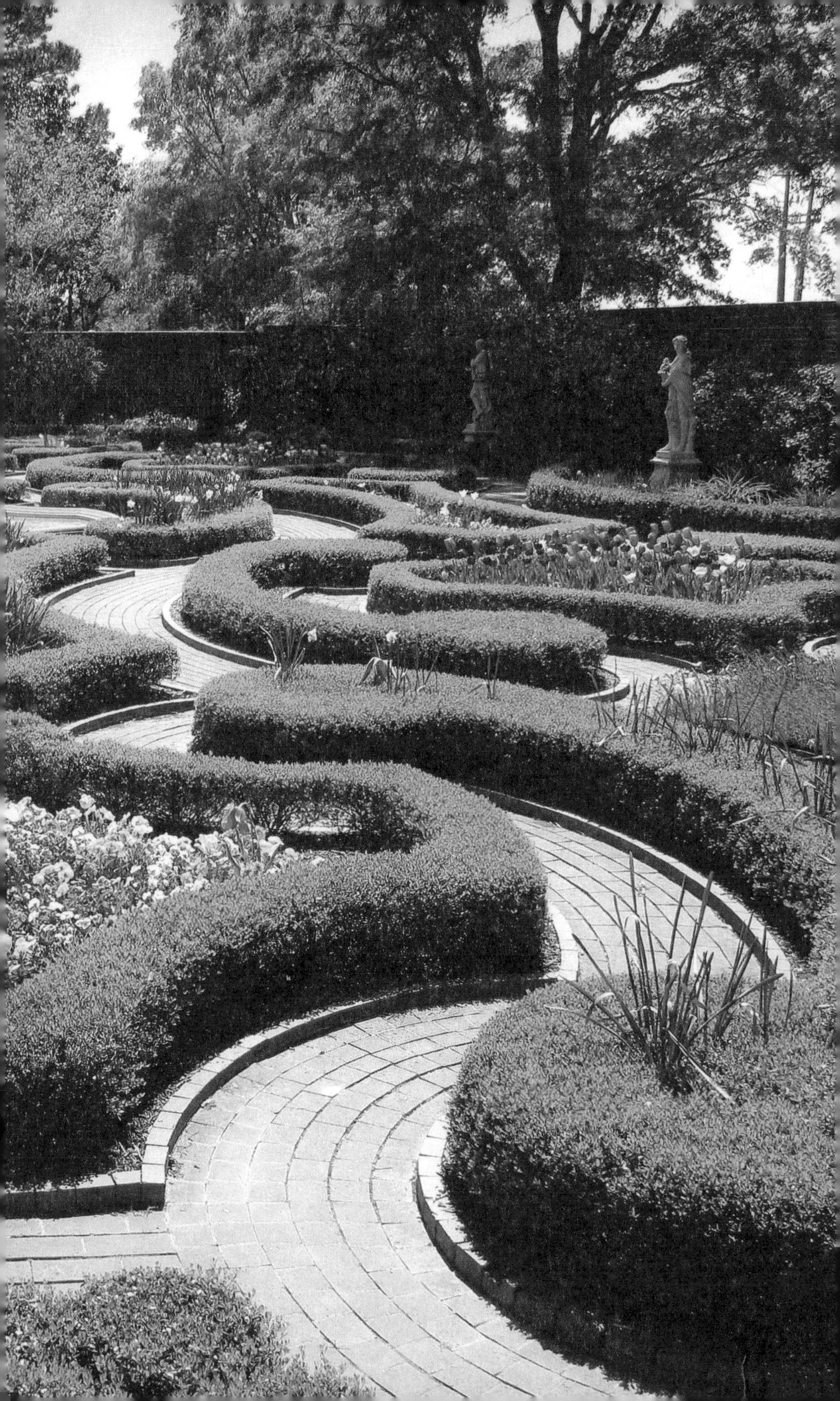

- 
- 

*Get help.* If you feel under-resourced, specifically when it comes to how you're able to relate and connect with people, I want you to get help. Consider joining a support group, getting therapy, or letting someone into your dilemma. They may not be able to fix your problem, but at least you won't be standing in your problem alone.

As you think of those areas in which you're under-resourced today, what are the extra supports you can access—this week—to help you grow and evolve?

_____

_____

_____

_____

_____

_____

## ACCESS GOD'S HELP

Spend some time talking to God about the areas in which you have very little.

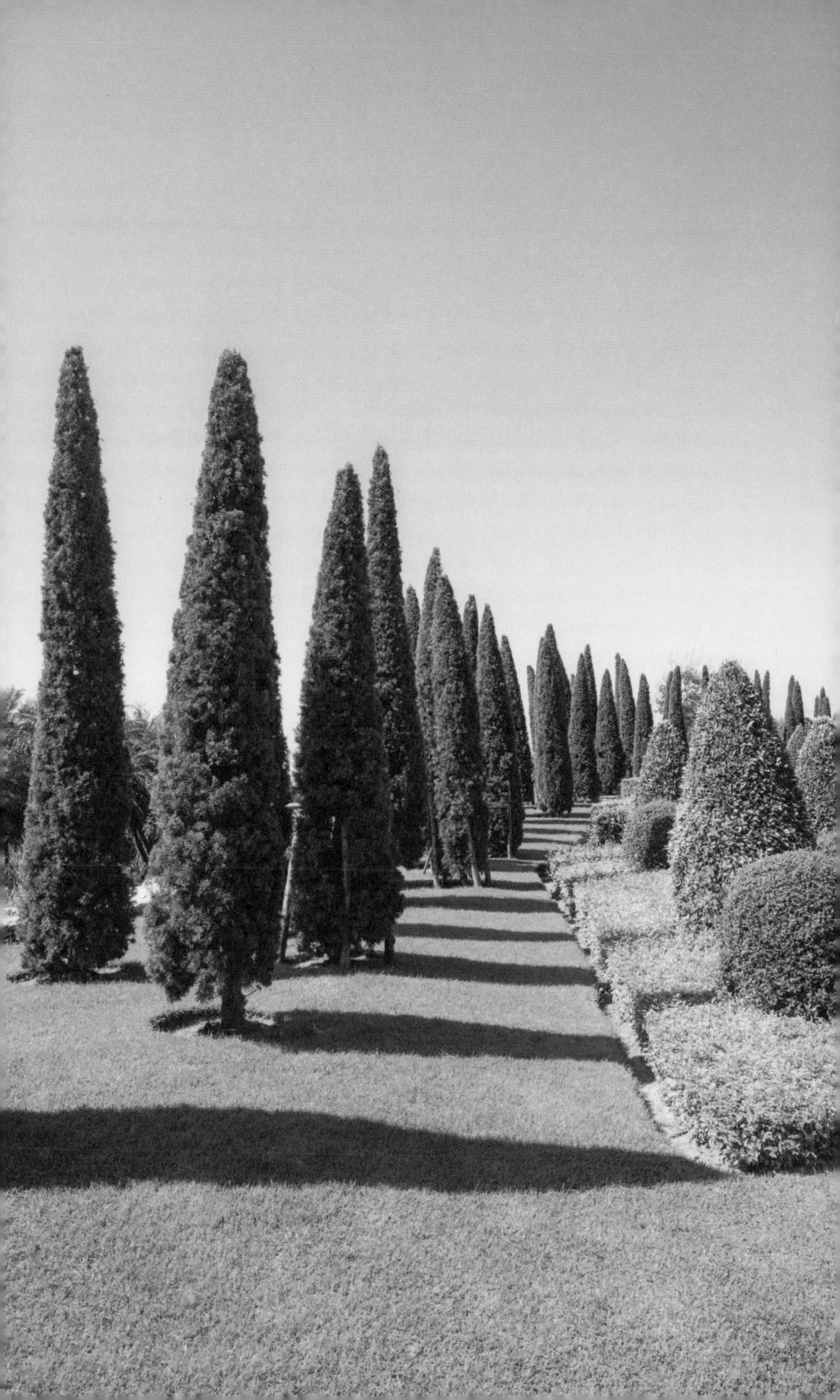

# HOW TO PRAY

Close your eyes and see yourself face-to-face with Jesus.

To His disciples, Jesus said, "You give them something to eat."

What is Jesus telling *you* to do, with His help, to serve His people?

_____

_____

_____

_____

_____

_____

Jesus' disciples said, "We have no more than five loaves and two fish." In what way(s) are you resisting Jesus' call on your life?

_____

_____

_____

_____

_____

What do you hear Jesus saying to you about your little bit that you have to offer?

_____

_____

_____

_____

_____

# INSPIRATION

The disciples didn't realize that when they were telling Jesus what they had in the boy's lunch, the little bit they had was every single thing they needed.

We know how this miracle ends. Jesus took the boy's little, the disciples' efforts, and His anointing, and a miracle took place. That's the sweet spot for us as believers. It's not when we're operating in our own strength and wisdom; it's when we come to a place where we combine our uncomfortable vulnerability with our under-resourced effort and lay it at Jesus' feet.

Never forget that God sees what you can't see. He knows the road ahead of you and the world around you. When you give Him something to work with, He gives you something worth the wait. I don't think there's anything that makes us more fragile than taking the most intimate pieces of our journey and turning them over to another.

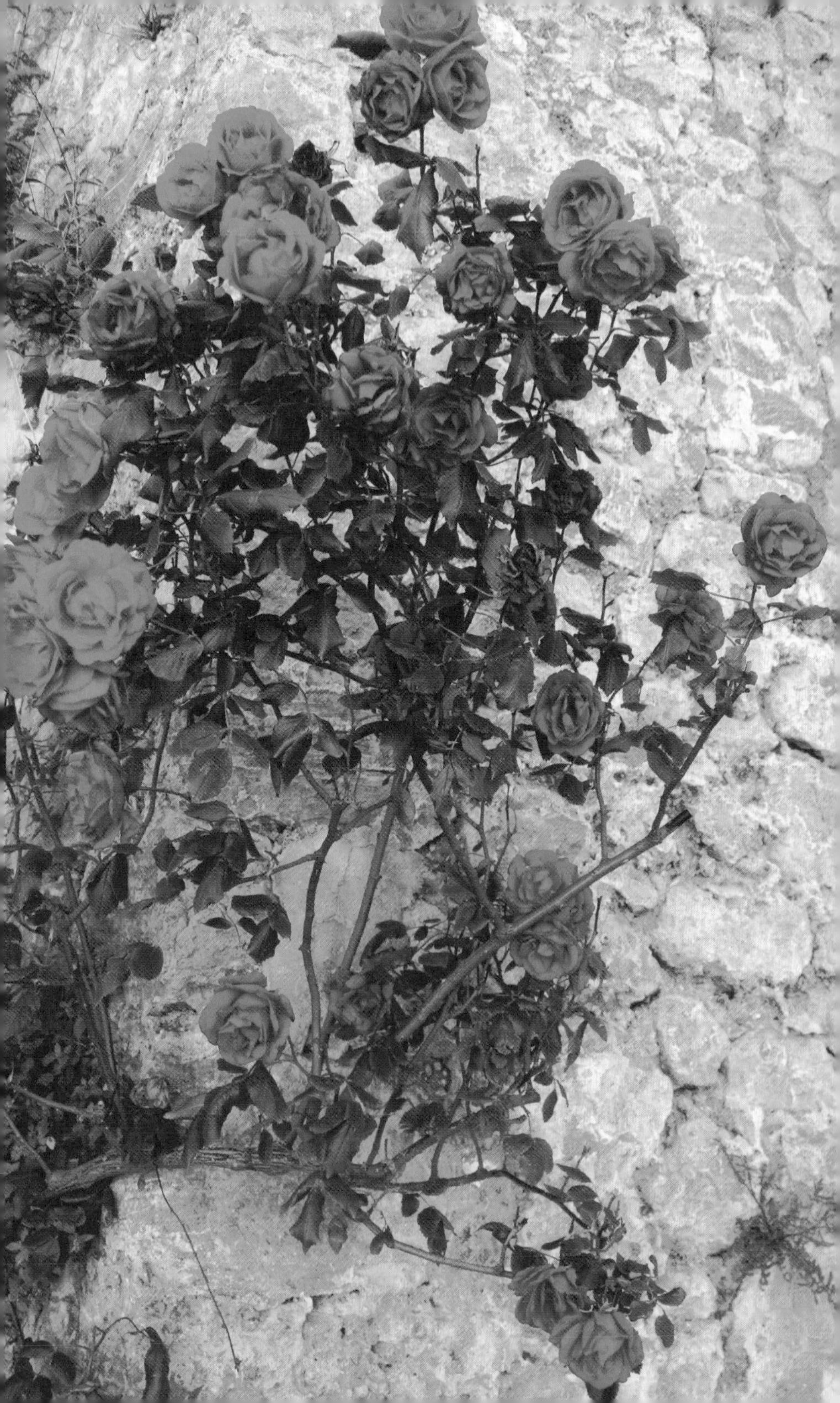

## MY PRAYER FOR YOU TODAY

---

*Heavenly Father, I ask that You give the woman reading this book the strength to open herself to You. Open her eyes to how You see her greatness and her sorrow. Grant her courage to stand up in the area where she's tempted to fall. Attract to her teachers, friends, community, and love that force her to raise her head and trust again. Help her to be comfortable in her own skin so the best of her can be multiplied for Your glory. Amen.*

---

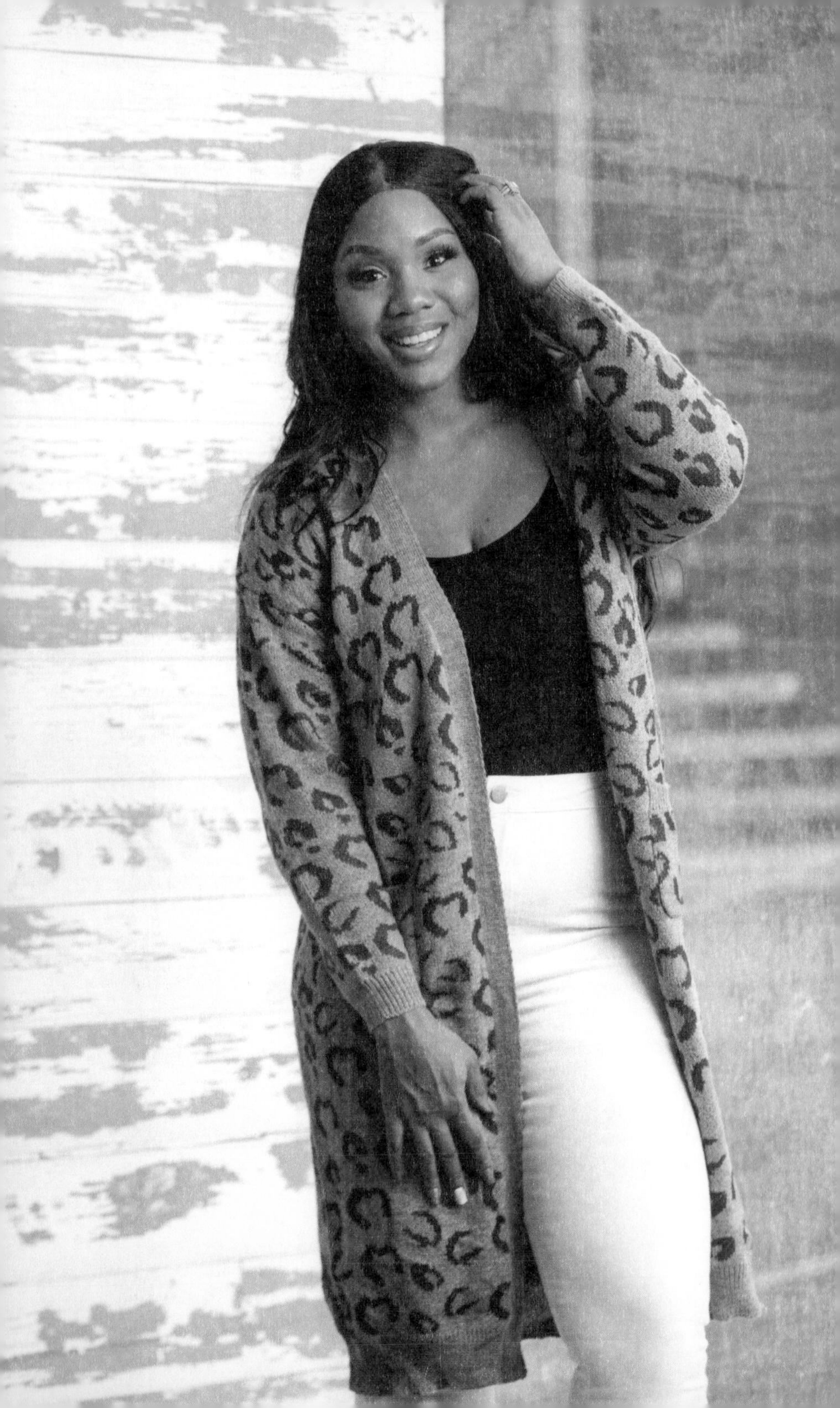

# CHAPTER SEVEN

# GOOD GOES HARD

*Then the man said, "The woman whom You gave*
*to be with me, she gave me of the tree, and I ate."*
—GENESIS 3:12

We talk so much about the euphoria and peace that come when we're in God's will, but I would not be responsible if I did not prepare you for the moments when good goes hard. You're going to make some decisions, and when you make those decisions, there are going to be some moments when you know you're in God's will. But sometimes you are also so tired and weary that you aren't sure whether or not you want to stay in God's will.

It's like when a woman makes the decision to be celibate, but then dating becomes a gazillion times harder. Or when you choose to quit the addiction, then realize you won't be able to hang out with your friends without being tempted. You choose to save money, but then you're no longer living the lifestyle you've become accustomed to. You thank God for the children, but the children are driving you crazy. The examples are countless, but the feelings are similar.

I think most of us subconsciously believe that surrendering our comfort and pursuing a life that allows God to lead us and guide us should guarantee peace, joy, loyalty, health, provision, and protection. We live with this in our subconscious, and when things happen that are in direct opposition to that belief, we become frustrated and hurt because we thought that our sacrifices would result in perpetual satisfaction. But good doesn't always equal easy, and easy doesn't always mean that it's good.

## WHEN THE BLESSING BECOMES THE NORM

The moment you begin to see the blessing as your norm, responsibility, or burden, the value begins to decrease because you no longer honor it as coming from God. So you have to be conscious that every good and perfect gift God gives you is received as the blessing it is. Consider the blessings in your life today—those listed below, and others—and pause to give God thanks for each one:

- your job
- your friend(s)
- your parent(s), living or dead, known to you or unknown

YOU WERE MADE TO OVERCOME

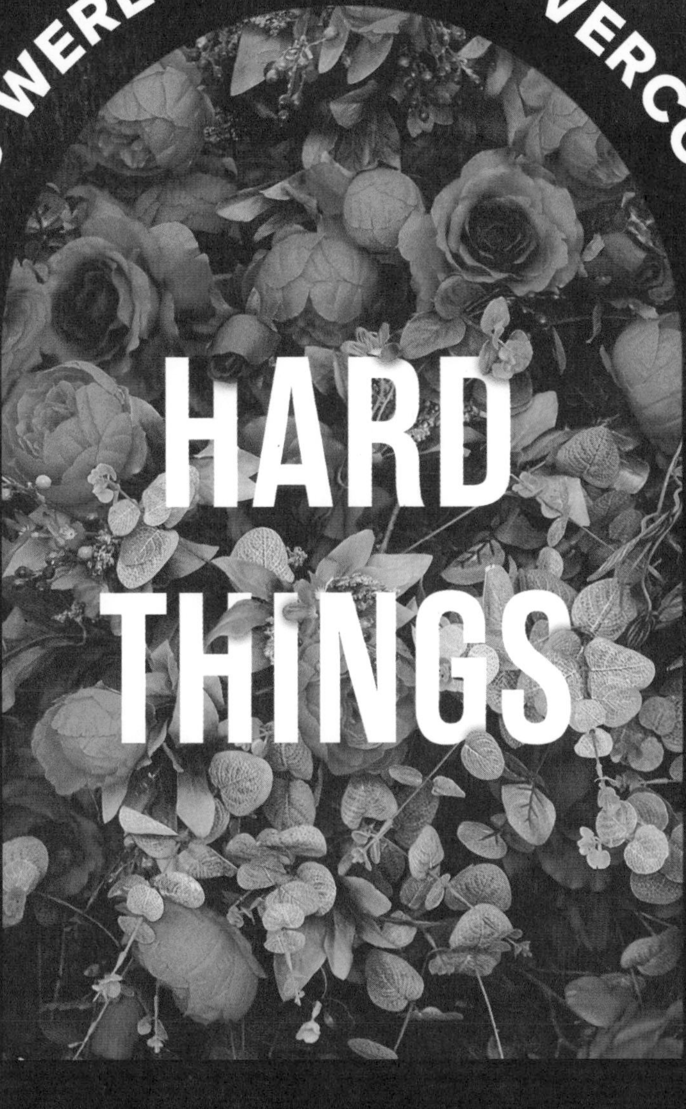
HARD
THINGS

- your sibling(s)
- your spouse, if you have one
- your child(ren), if you have any
- your school, if you have one
- your church
- your home
- your health
- your respite or vacation
- your relationship with God
- your _____

## BLESSING OR BURDEN?

What area of your life feels like a burden but started off as a blessing?

_____

_____

_____

_____

_____

What was happening in your life at the time this blessing arrived that made you feel fortunate to have it?

_____

_____

_____

_____

_____

When was the first time you began to feel like your
blessing was a burden?

_____

_____

_____

_____

When was the last time that blessing felt like a blessing?

_____

_____

_____

_____

Now look at what you wrote. Sometimes you need to back
away from your blessing so you can see it properly. There may
be some areas where you could have been a better steward

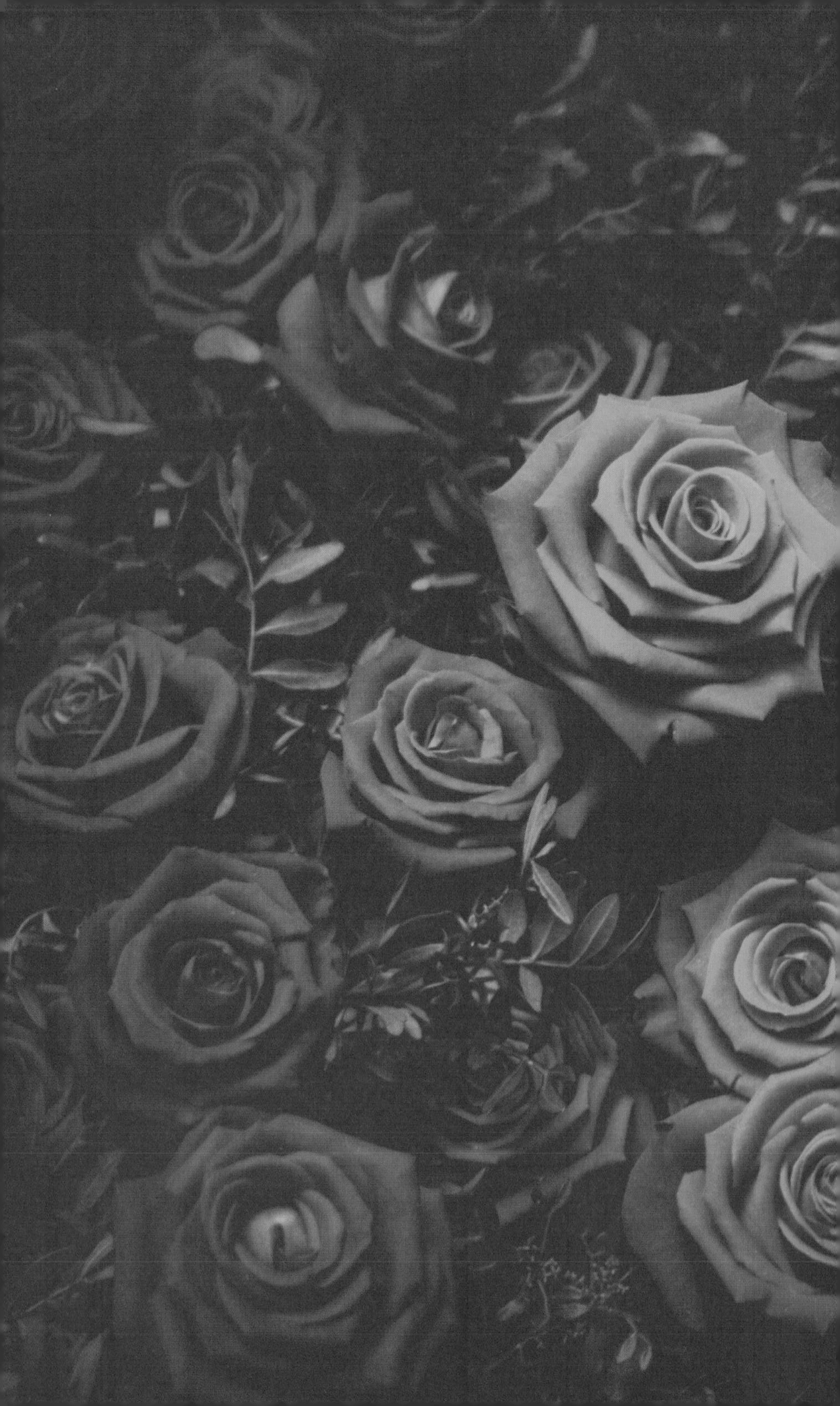

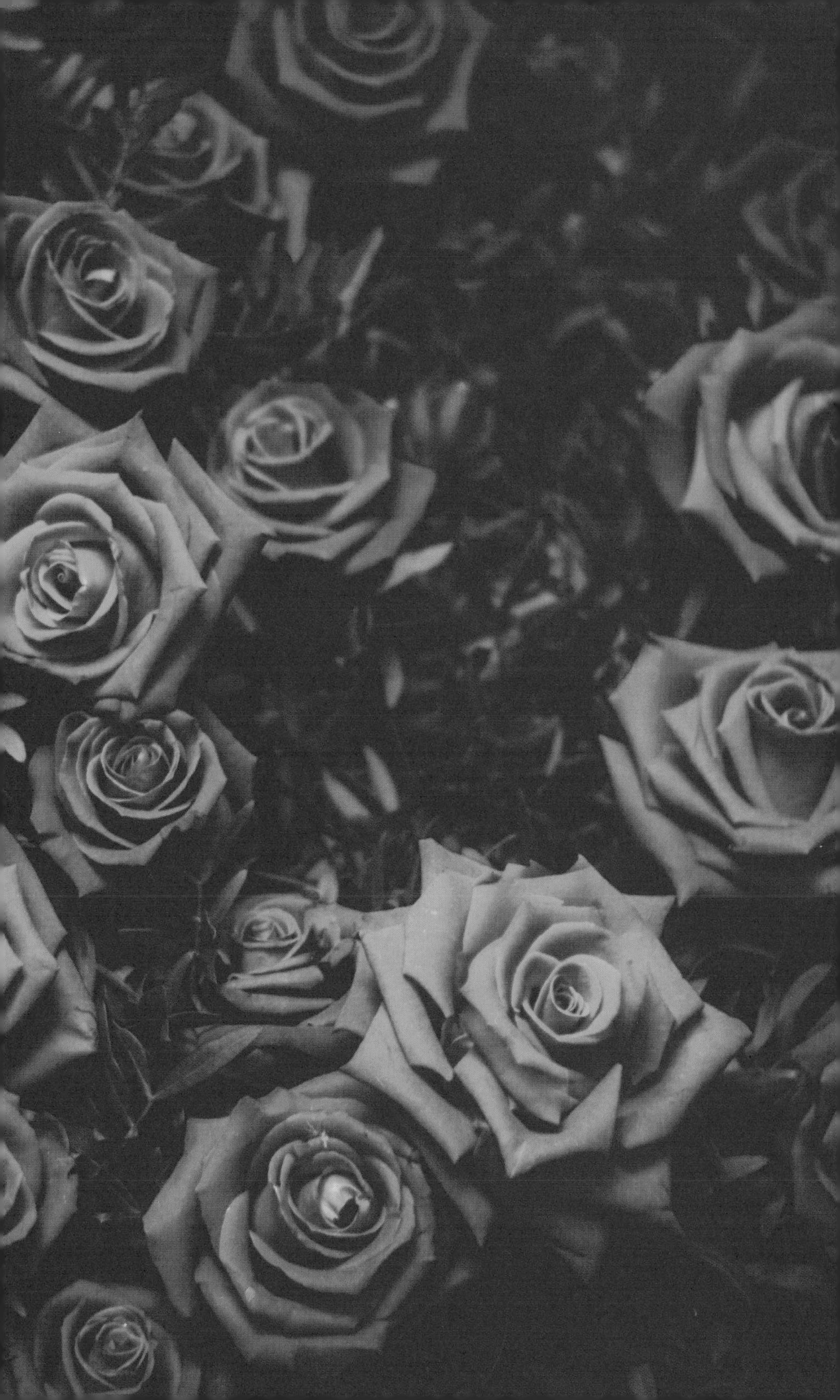

over your blessing, or maybe as the blessing unfolded, you experienced some surprises that detracted from the honor you had for the blessing.

Is there something you need to accept, reject, or change that is clouding your vision of that blessing?

## YOU MATTER

Your soul matters. Your mental health matters. Your body matters. Your peace matters. Your feelings matter. You can't expect other people to see you as a priority if you don't see yourself as one.

Begin to consider what self-care and soul-care look like in your life. Self-care may be something that makes you feel good afterward but doesn't actually give you peace in the moment (for example, exercise that feels hard, or healthy veggies with a bad aftertaste). And soul-care is what feeds your spirit, leaving you feeling rested and relaxed. For example, soul-care for me is meditation, reading a book, or sleeping. Both self-care and soul-care are important to being balanced.

Start a self-care / soul-care match with someone close to you. The goal is to do one thing a day that is self-care / soul-care. At the end of each day, make a list of what you did that day for *you*!

Who's the person you'll invite to share this holy routine with you?

To practice, think about yesterday. How did you practice soul-care? How did you practice self-care?

_____

_____

_____

_____

_____

If you failed to care for you yesterday, what will you do differently today?

_____

_____

_____

_____

_____

## ACCESS GOD'S HELP

When good goes hard, it's meant to force you to stop functioning the way you were so you can create new rhythms and paradigms. Innovation is the product of frustration.

Where are you frustrated today? What is not working in

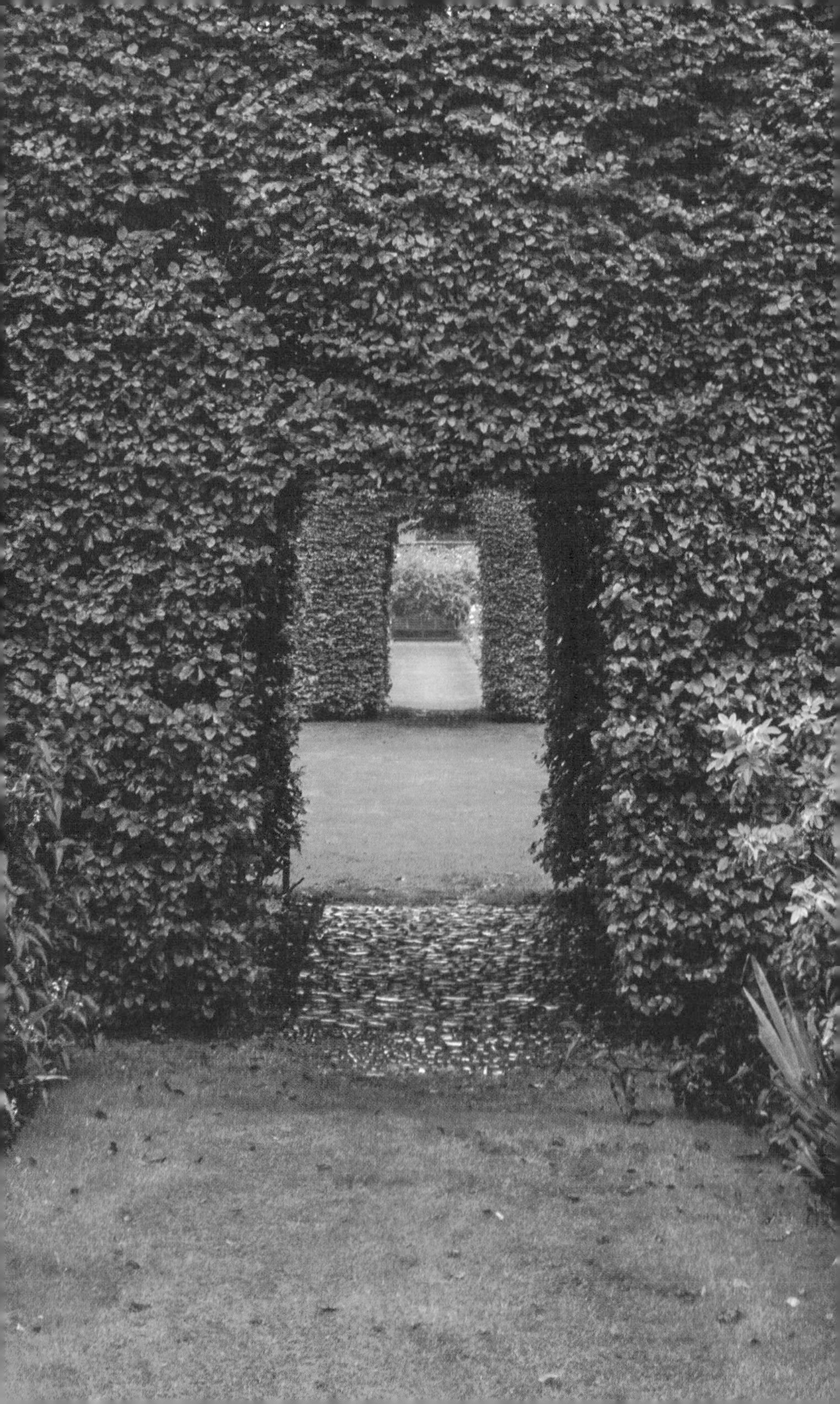

your life? Offer these areas of your life to God by jotting them down here.

_____

_____

_____

_____

_____

_____

# HOW TO PRAY

Consider if there is a better way to function that you don't currently see. Ask God to show you a better way. Is there a way to tweak the way your life's rhythm has been functioning?

Take your time. Listen for God's voice, and then note, here, what God is speaking to your heart.

_____

_____

_____

_____

_____

_____

## INSPIRATION

Moses is my third favorite person in the Bible (Jesus and Eve hold the first two spots). Did you know before Moses answered the call to be a deliverer that he left Egypt and began to live a comfortable life (Exodus 2:21–22)? Had Moses stayed away from the place where he experienced frustration, he never would have discovered what God placed inside him. He would have ultimately been living unfulfilled because he wasn't living out God's dream for his life. I don't want you to miss out on getting to know you. You may be thinking that you're better off on the sidelines, not making any waves—but you're also not realizing that God sees you as a force.

Don't let the hard things trick you. You're stronger than you believe. You don't have to suppress your emotions and pretend you're okay when you're really not feeling strong. You are a real, vulnerable, authentic, confident, revolutionary world-changer who is strong because of who she is, not because of who she pretends to be. The quicker you learn how to harness your power and balance who you are, the sooner you can get to the business of exploring the depths of the strength God has placed in you. You were made to overcome hard things. When good goes hard, you go harder!

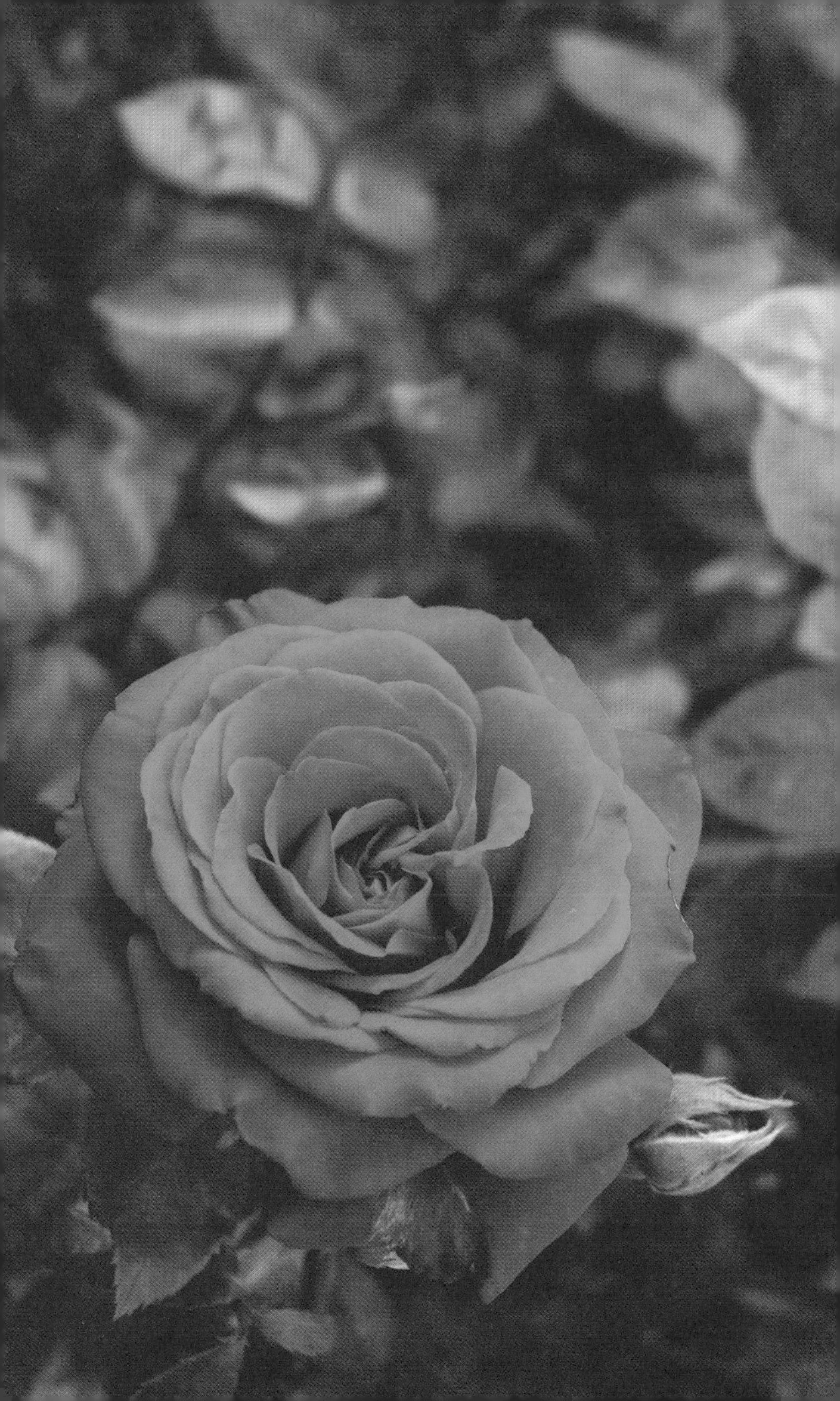

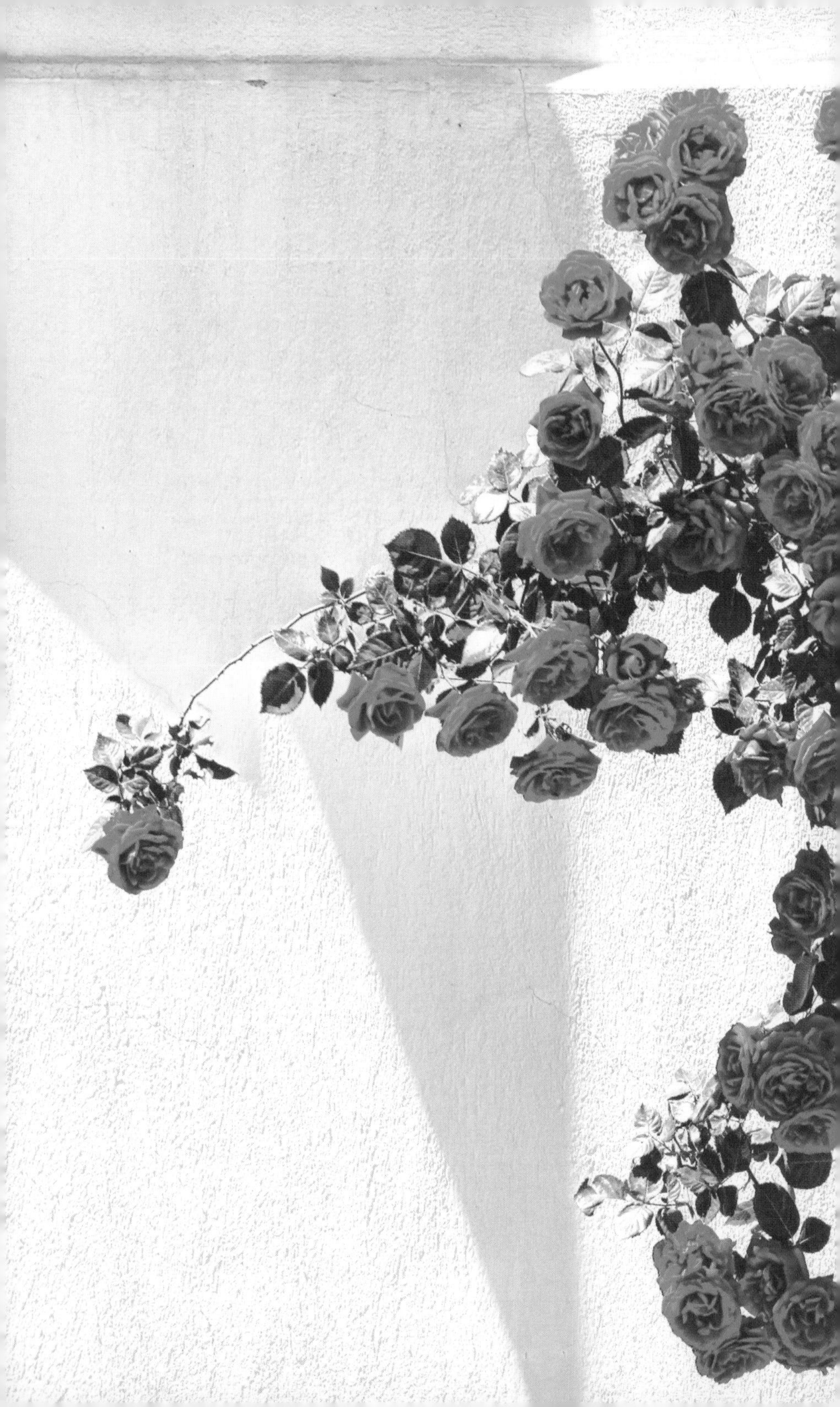

# MY PRAYER FOR YOU TODAY

---

*Father, by Your Holy Spirit, remind my sister that she is a force to be reckoned with! Help her to see herself as You see her: someone who deserves the kind of care she so freely offers others. Open her eyes to those places where she is weary, stuck, burdened, and frustrated. And then invite her to find refreshment by sitting in Your presence. Nourish her with Your Word and help her to practice the kinds of self-care and soul-care that will revive her body, mind, soul, and spirit. I ask You in the strong name of Jesus, amen.*

---

# CHAPTER EIGHT

# GOD GOALS

*And Peter answered Him and said, "Lord, if it is*
*You, command me to come to You on the water."*
—MATTHEW 14:28

Have you heard the story about Peter, one of Jesus' disciples, attempting to walk on water? Jesus commanded Peter to come to Him, and for a split second Peter began to walk on the water. Unfortunately he took his eyes off Jesus, and the moment he did, he began to sink. Fortunately for Peter, Jesus was there to save him (Matthew 14:28–32). Peter may not have completed the task the way he had in mind, but he did accomplish something he would have never accomplished had he not challenged himself in the first place.

I want you to begin making goals for yourself without fear of failure or of the unknown. Strive to come to a place where you are content with starting to head in the right direction, and don't get caught up in whether you'll reach the desired destination.

If our goal is to become more and more like the image of our Creator, we're going to have to step out of what we know and begin seeking out what God knows.

Peter got back in the boat. Peter kept walking with the disciples. Peter kept connecting with the world around him, but he was not the same Peter he was before he stepped out of the boat. Peter and Jesus had an insider understanding that only the two of them knew.

Maybe you just need to step away from your circle long enough to get some inside information about who God is and what God can do with you.

## IDENTIFY YOUR GOALS

I'm inviting you to think about your life and create goals that fit within three specific categories:

- short-term goals
- long-term goals
- generational goals

Get big, bad, and bold in your dreaming. List whatever comes to your mind. As you do, notice that your short-term goals determine whether you'll accomplish your long-term goals. Similarly, your generational goals depend on you accomplishing your long-term goals.

Begin by noticing your now. What are you accomplishing today? What do you want to do with your tomorrow? Identify the short-term goals you want to accomplish within the coming months.

Short-term goals

_____

_____

_____

_____

_____

What are the long-term goals you want to accomplish in the coming years and decades?

Long-term goals

_____

_____

_____

_____

_____

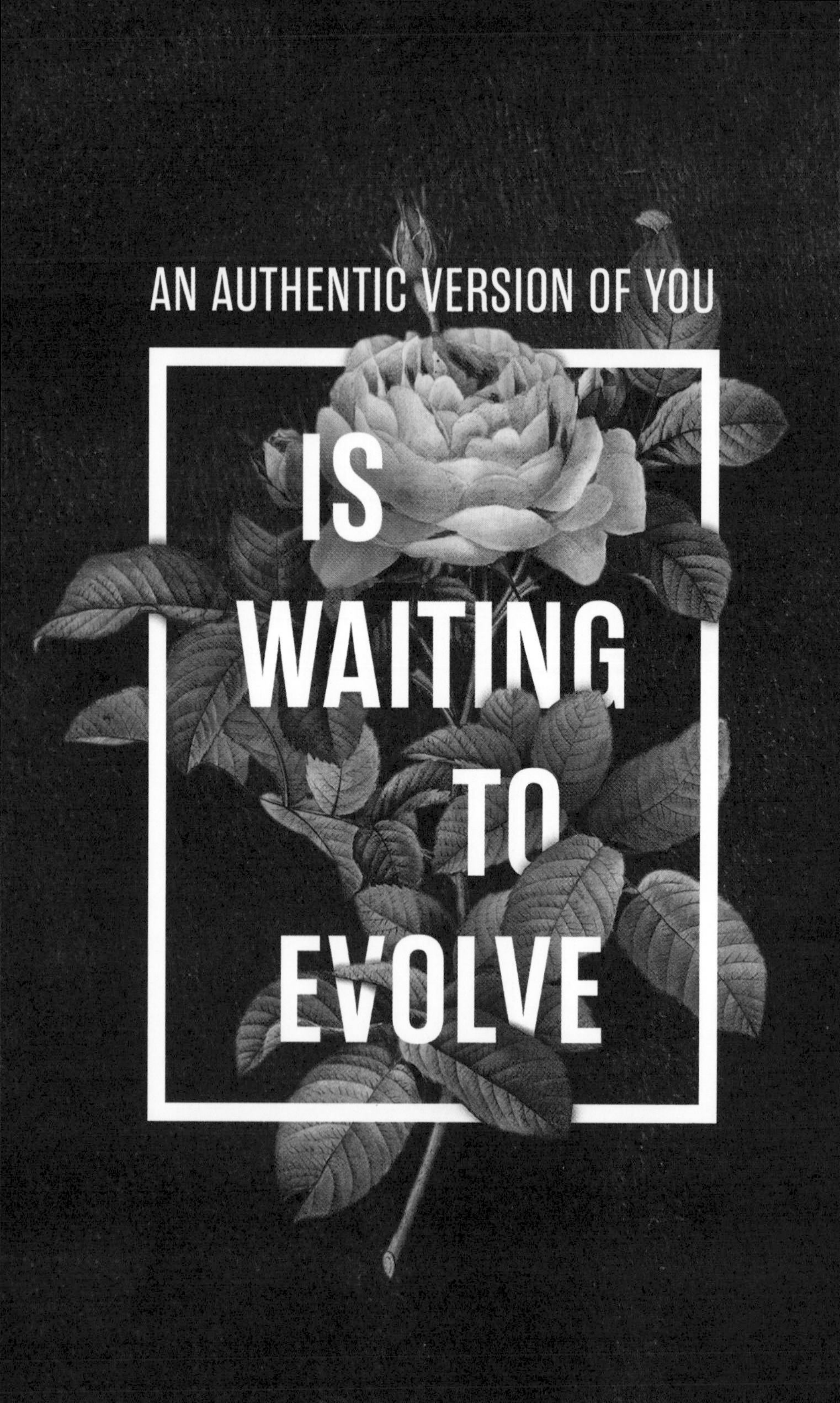
AN AUTHENTIC VERSION OF YOU
IS
WAITING
TO
EVOLVE

Generational goals are a way to recognize that your life is bigger than you, and what you do each day doesn't just affect you—it affects the generation that is alive to see your journey. This goal will become the new way of existing for the people who are exposed to your journey. That could be family, friends, coworkers, and/or mentees whom you desire to be exposed to a new model.

What are your generational goals?

Generational goals

_____

_____

_____

_____

_____

_____

_____

_____

After you've identified the goals you want to be pursuing in the next months and years, do a little reverse engineering. Start with one of your generational goals, and notice what it will take for you to reach it.

Is there a long-term goal that helps you reach your generational goal?

_____

_____

_____

_____

_____

_____

_____

Is there a short-term goal that helps you reach your long-term goal?

_____

_____

_____

_____

_____

_____

_____

_____

# MAKE IT BITE-SIZED

Examine your personal goals again. Can you take your short-term goals and begin to make them bite-sized and manageable? Brainstorm the smaller steps you need to take to achieve your short-term goals here:

_____

_____

_____

_____

_____

_____

_____

_____

_____

_____

_____

_____

_____

_____

_____

### A Note from Sarah

The hardest part is getting started! But all you really must do is sit back and allow the inevitable outcome of sticking to your goals to show up in your life.

# LISTENING FOR THE WORD THAT MATTERS MOST

Receiving a word from God is different from receiving a word from man, although God can use man to deliver His word. When you receive a word from God, it bypasses your mind and hits you in your soul. It's a word that brings a part of you to life that you didn't know existed. If you've ever been through a hard time and had friends try to lend support or encouraging words, some of them sounded routine, but every now and then a word moves beyond your feelings and emotions and lands right in your soul. That word is the word God placed enough weight on that it broke through your walls.

In the past, when have you received a word—from Scripture, or through the lips of a person, or whispered in your ear by the Spirit—that you knew was from God? When did God's word land right in your soul?

_____

_____

_____

_____

_____

_____

_____

_____

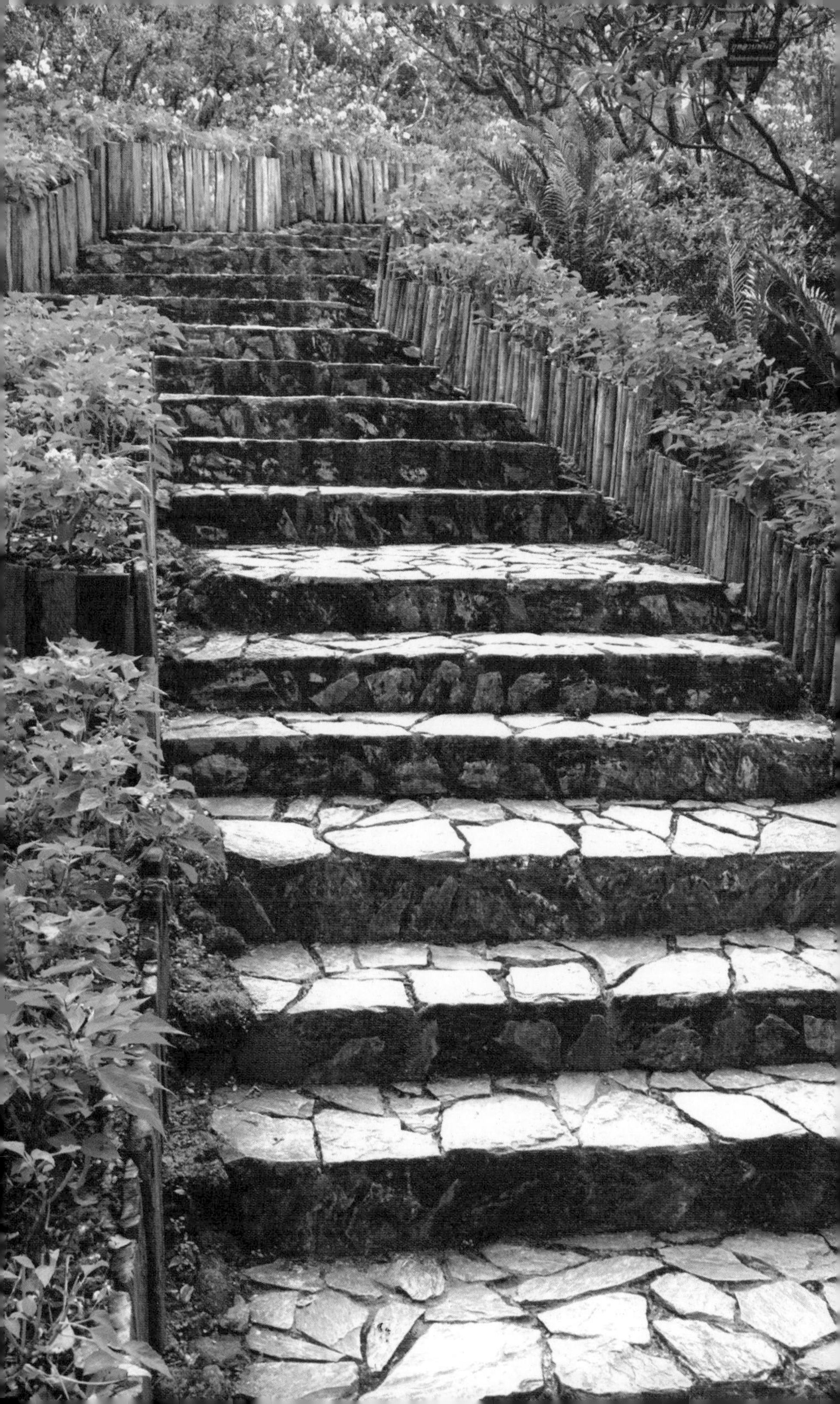

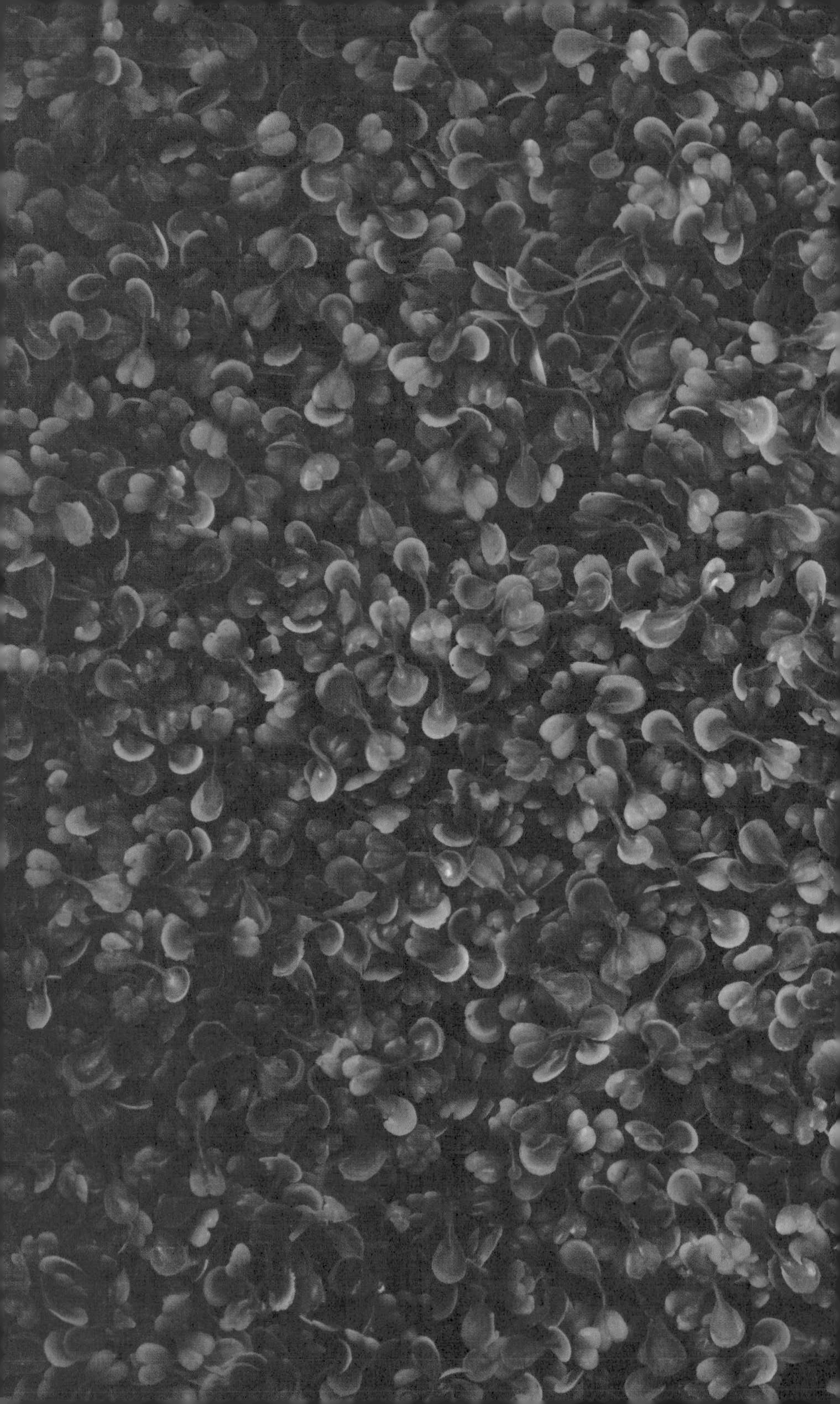

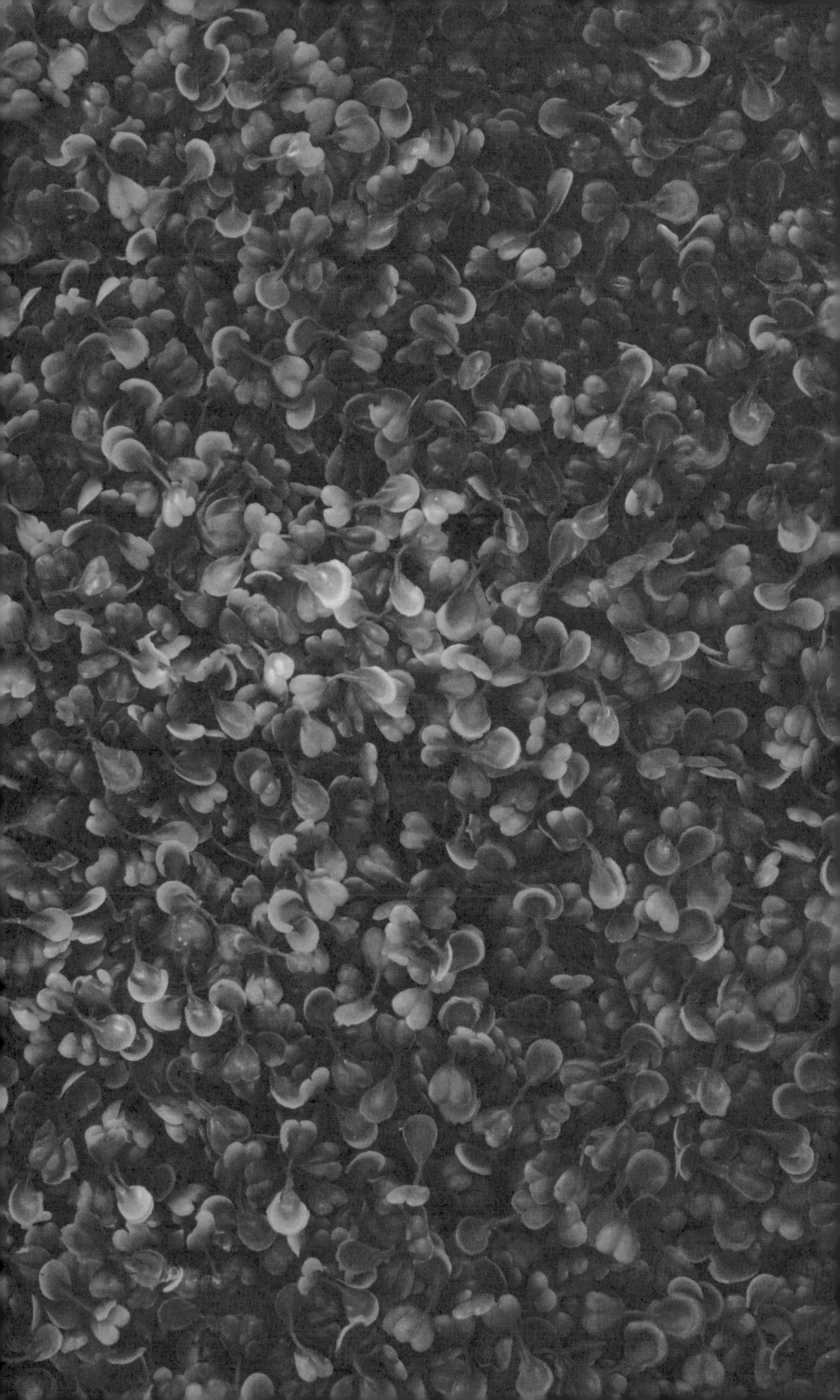

## ACCESS GOD'S HELP

What is God speaking to you about your destiny? Have you paused to listen? Set apart some time to spend in quiet listening this week. Specifically, bring your goals before God and listen for His affirmation, adjustment, and guidance.

## HOW TO PRAY

This kind of listening prayer is prayer that is unhurried. We don't control when or what or how God speaks to us, but we can position ourselves to assume a listening posture.

In the Old Testament, the seasoned priest Eli coached his young charge Samuel how to listen for God's voice. Eli told Samuel, "Go and lie down, and if he calls you, say, 'Speak, LORD, for your servant is listening'" (1 Samuel 3:9 NIV).

> ### A Note from Sarah
>
> The word that you received from God is worth hanging on to! The Enemy will try to snatch that word you received, so it is your job to protect it and honor it. Capturing it here is one way to do that.

After setting apart all the time you need, having a pen and this guided journal at your fingertips, offer your goals to God.

- God, I offer You the short-term goals in my heart. Speak, Lord, for Your servant is listening.

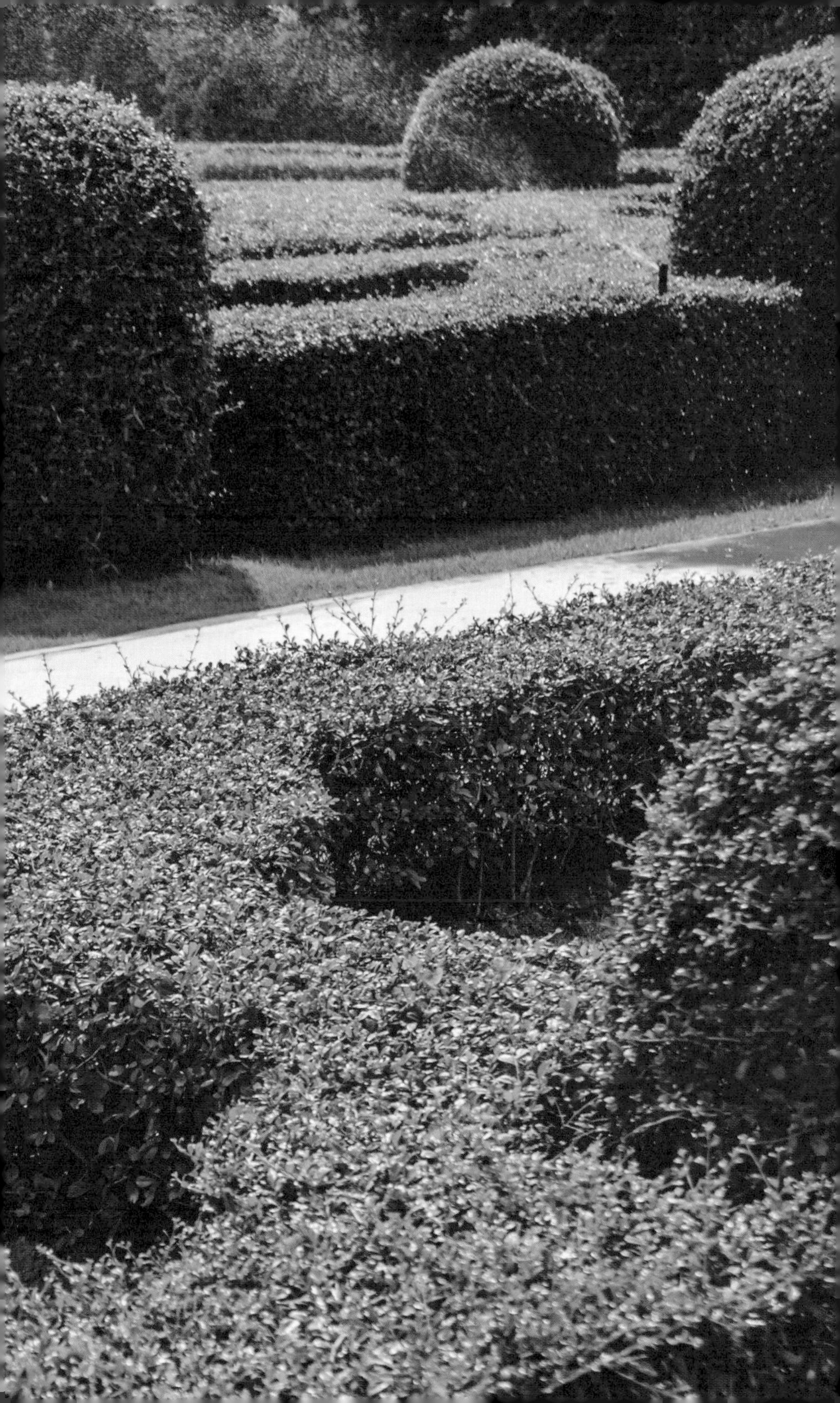

- God, I offer You the long-term goals in my heart. Speak, Lord, for Your servant is listening.
- God, I offer You the generational goals in my heart. Speak, Lord, for Your servant is listening.

**Without judgment, jot down whatever you notice.**

_____

_____

_____

_____

_____

## INSPIRATION

### A Note from Sarah

Sometimes God speaks to us in the time we've allotted for listening. And God may choose to speak to us in unexpected moments as well! Keep your ears tuned to God's frequency so that you can receive whatever it is God is speaking to your heart.

When God revealed that seed would lead to victory in Genesis 3:15, Eve developed tunnel vision about the seed. The seed was going to be what restored her confidence. The seed was going to be what gave her back her power and authority. The seed was going to drown out the voices of shame, regret, and disappointment. The word that God gave Eve specifically was directly connected to her producing biologically. It may or may not be necessary to say that not every seed is about biological production. Some seeds are about books; ministry; nonprofits; business; education; relationships; mental, emotional, and/or spiritual health. We have the seed God gives to all humanity, and then we have our specific seed.

Are you ready to work the seeds God has given you? Has God given you a word regarding your destiny? Like Eve, God is inviting you to work the goal of bringing what He has said to manifestation.

## MY PRAYER FOR YOU TODAY

*Creator God, Giver of life, You have planted seeds of hope and purpose and destiny within the woman who is reading these words. Open her eyes to see what You have for her. Open her ears to hear Your voice speaking to her heart. Quicken her mind and strengthen her arms to accomplish what it is that You have destined for her: hour by hour, day by day, year by year. Help her to hang on tight to what You have spoken and continue to honor what You've put inside her. I ask this in Jesus' name and for His glory. Amen.*

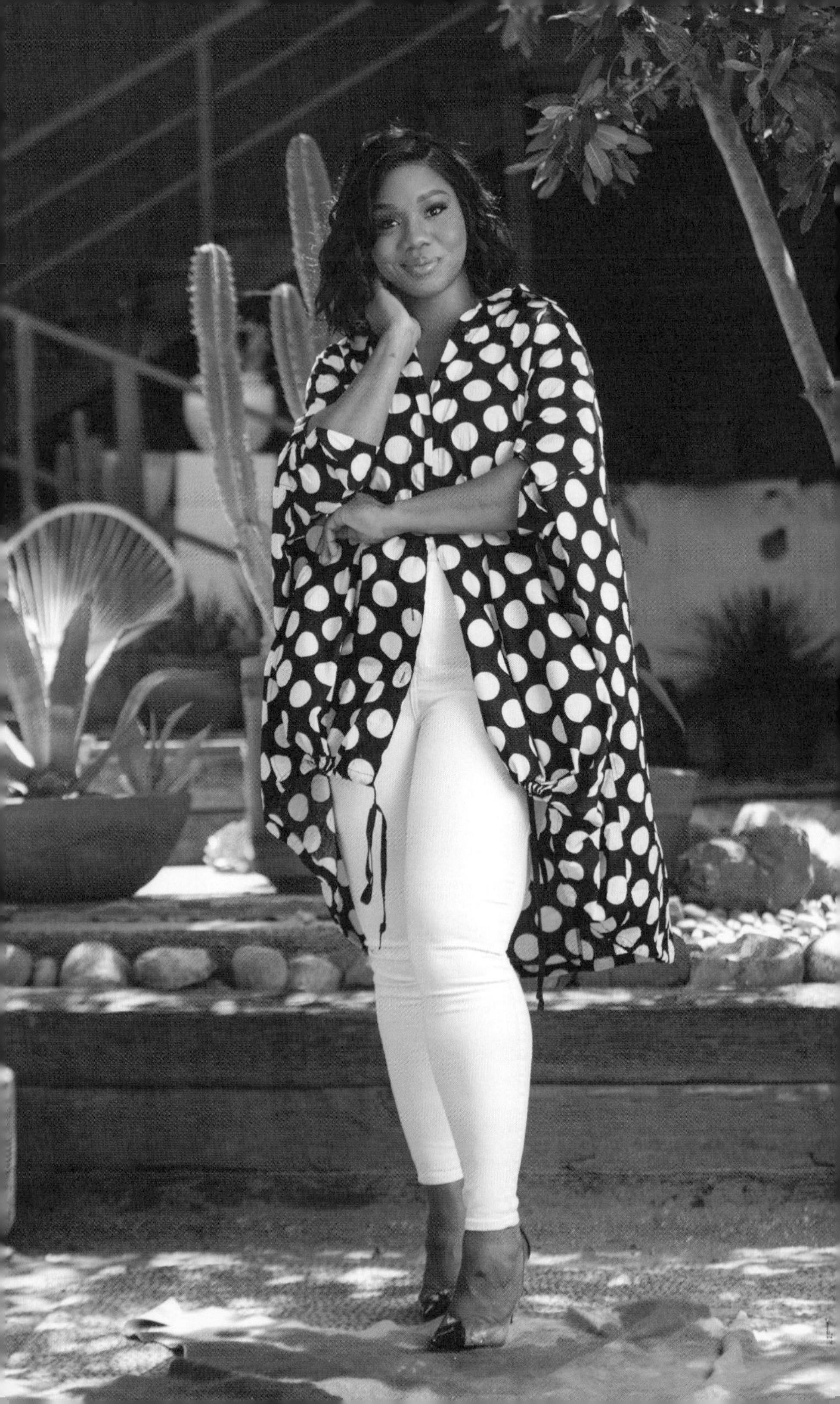

# CHAPTER NINE

# SET IT IN MOTION

> *Adam knew his wife again, and she bore a son and named him Seth, "For God has appointed another seed for me instead of Abel, whom Cain killed." And as for Seth, to him also a son was born; and he named him Enosh. Then men began to call on the name of the LORD.*
>
> —GENESIS 4:25–26

When we meet a short-term goal, the long-term goal keeps us motivated. But if things happened overnight, there would be no need for discipline.

*Discipline* is about coming to a place where we no longer feel entitled to outcomes but rather expect them because they are the organic product of the effort we expend each day. It's the most underrated character trait. By the way, it's easy to require a character trait from another person when it's one that we've mastered ourselves, but when we aren't sure that we possess it, we'd rather not mention it at all. I feel like this is how we handle discipline.

No one is entirely sure how well they can discipline themselves until they actually try to do it. For instance, I may be disciplined when it comes to one thing but struggling in another area. I'm learning that discipline is not a state, but rather a process of correction. When we lack discipline, what we're actually lacking is the ability to correct the patterns we know should change. We have an outcome in mind, but the outcome is not attainable without discipline. And discipline cannot come without correction.

## DISCIPLINE

Sometimes people are trying to correct us, but we're too fragile to receive the correction, so we push it away. When we push it away, we fail to realize that we're also pushing away the outcome that will help to further manifest our journey. Discipline is about fine-tuning the outcome.

Is there a goal you have today that you are not meeting because you lack discipline?

_____

_____

_____

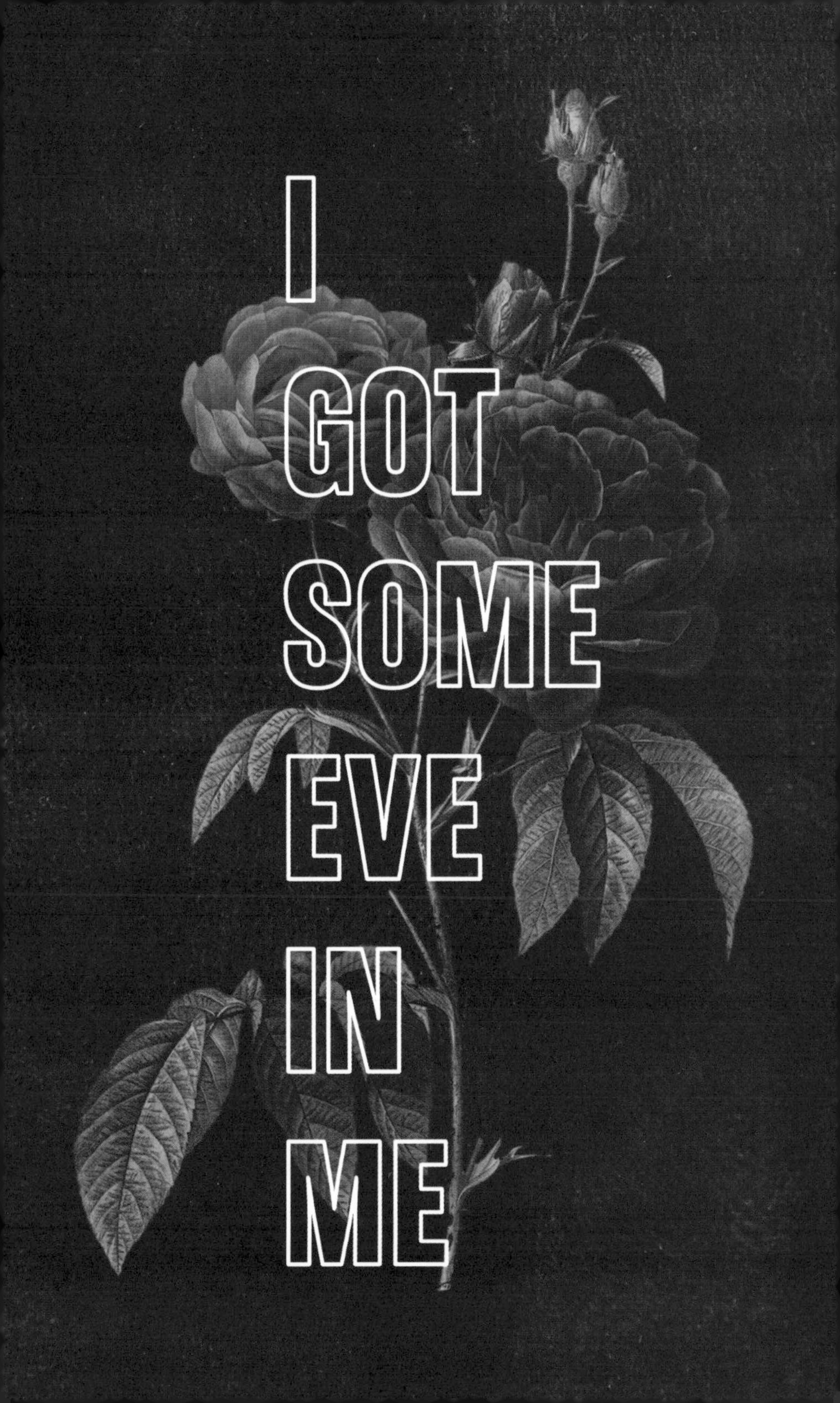
I
GOT
SOME
EVE
IN
ME

_____

_____

What is one example in your life where you met a goal because you exercised discipline?

_____

_____

_____

_____

What do you think caused the example you just shared to be successful?

_____

_____

_____

_____

_____

## CRITICISM VERSUS CORRECTION

Discipline cannot come without correction.

Have you ever considered the way that you give and receive correction?

There is a difference between criticism and correction. *Criticism* has a tinge of meanness connected to it and often comes from a person who may not have your best interests at heart. *Correction* is when someone loves you so much that they want to make you aware of a tendency you have that could be limiting your growth.

Jot down particular moments in your journey when you received or offered criticism or correction:

| | I RECEIVED IT . . . | I GAVE IT . . . |
|---|---|---|
| Criticism | | |
| Correction | | |

## WHEN WE'RE WRONG

Let's take a deeper look at how you receive and give correction. Maybe you're not like me and you don't struggle with receiving correction, but you have been accused of being a little rough in giving correction. Your intentions are good, but could your delivery be better?

*Jot down the last time you were wrong.* How did you learn you were wrong? How did it make you feel? Angry?

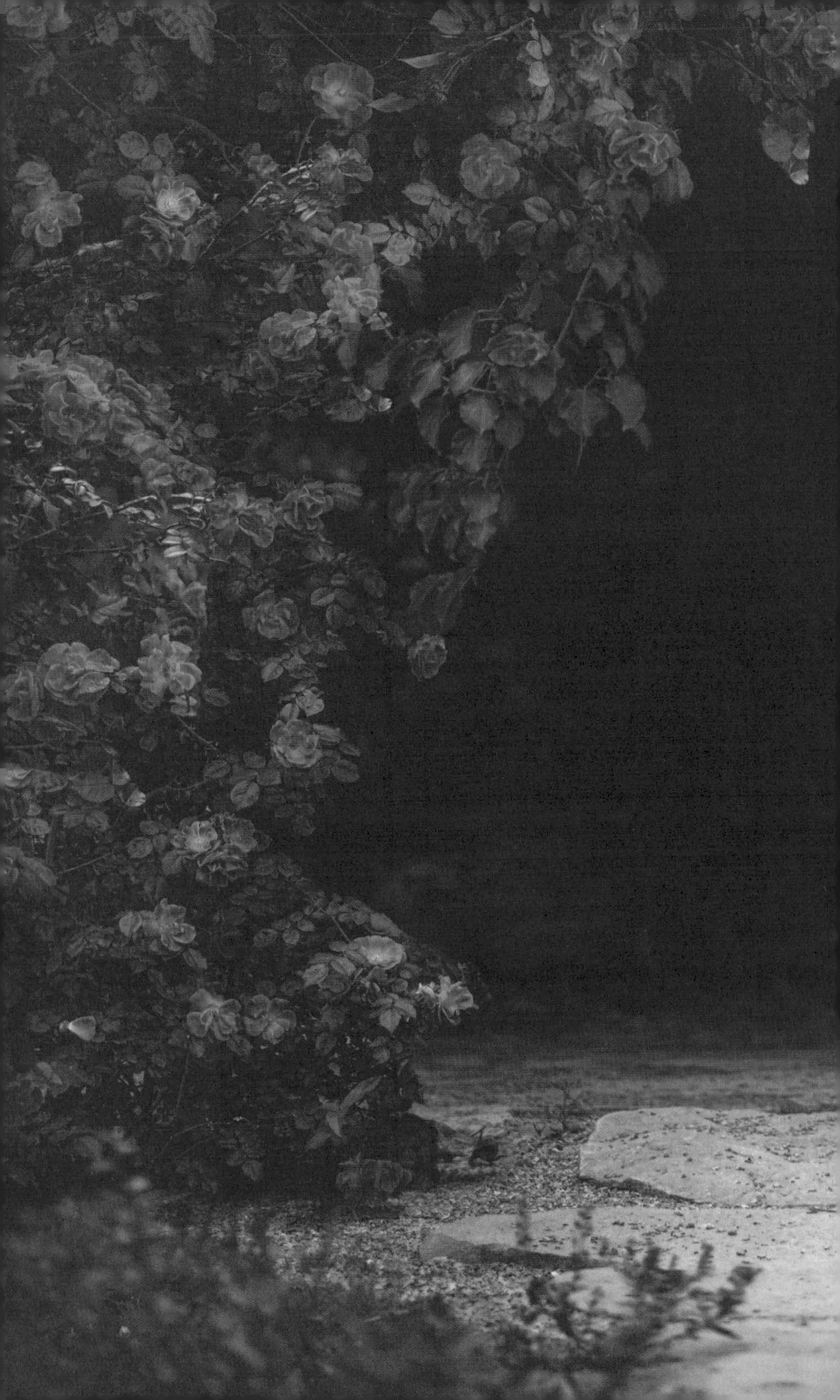

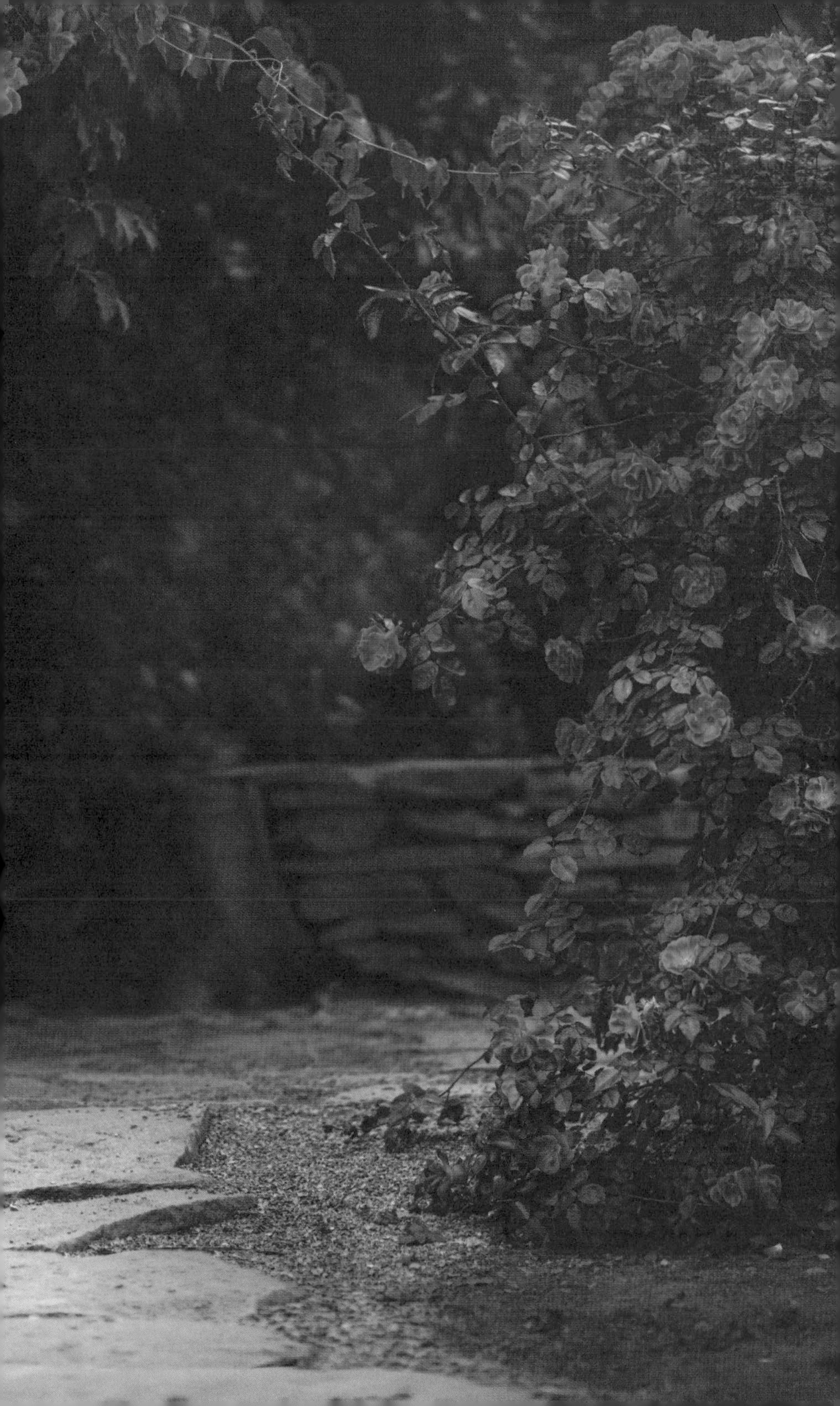

Ashamed? Hurt? Misunderstood? What would you have done differently armed with the knowledge you now have? Did you apologize to the person affected by your decision? Note: There's nothing wrong with being wrong. Having the ability to acknowledge and fix your wrongs builds trust.

_____

_____

_____

_____

_____

_____

*Consider how you would have preferred to hear that you were wrong.* How would you have preferred to receive correction from another?

_____

_____

_____

_____

_____

_____

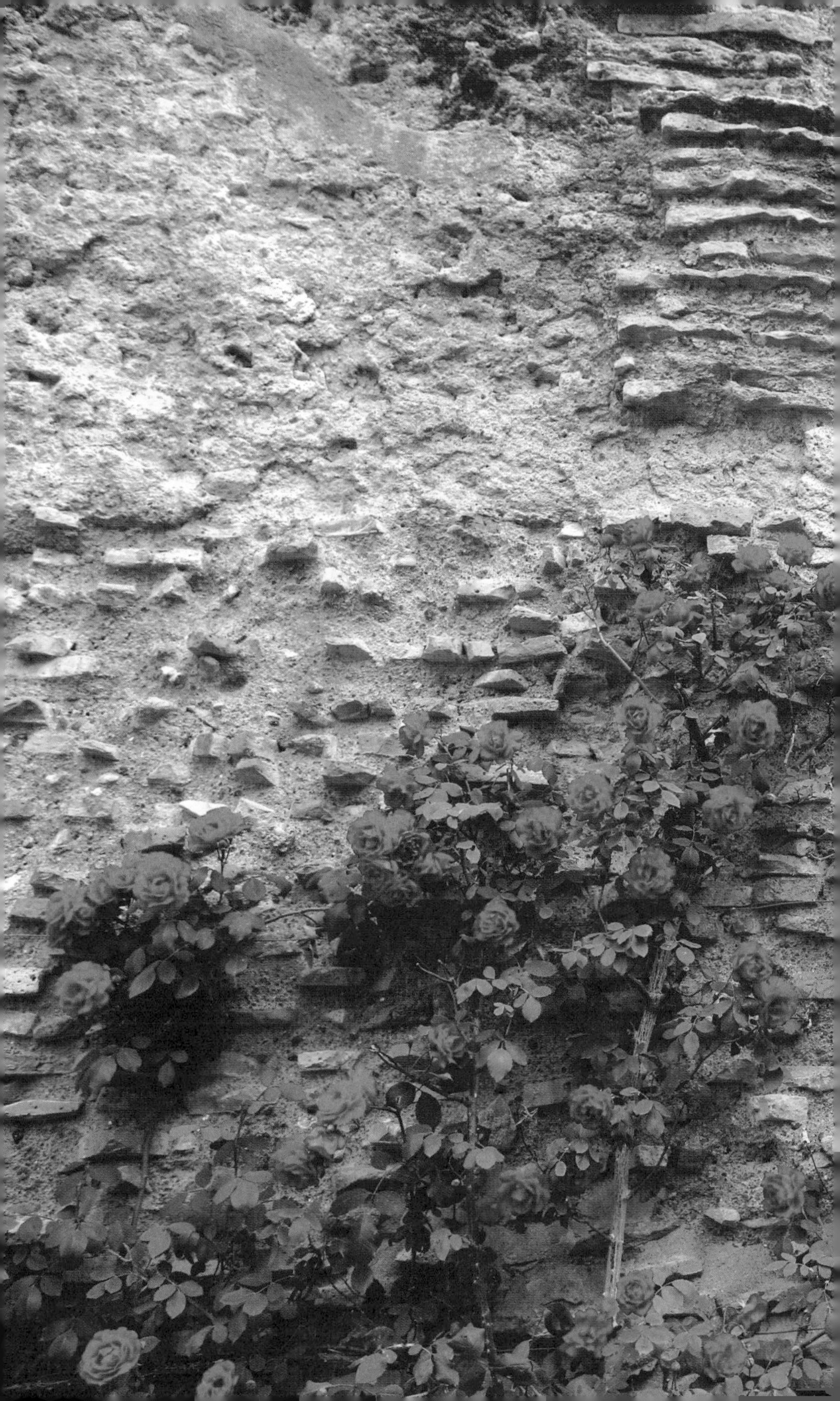

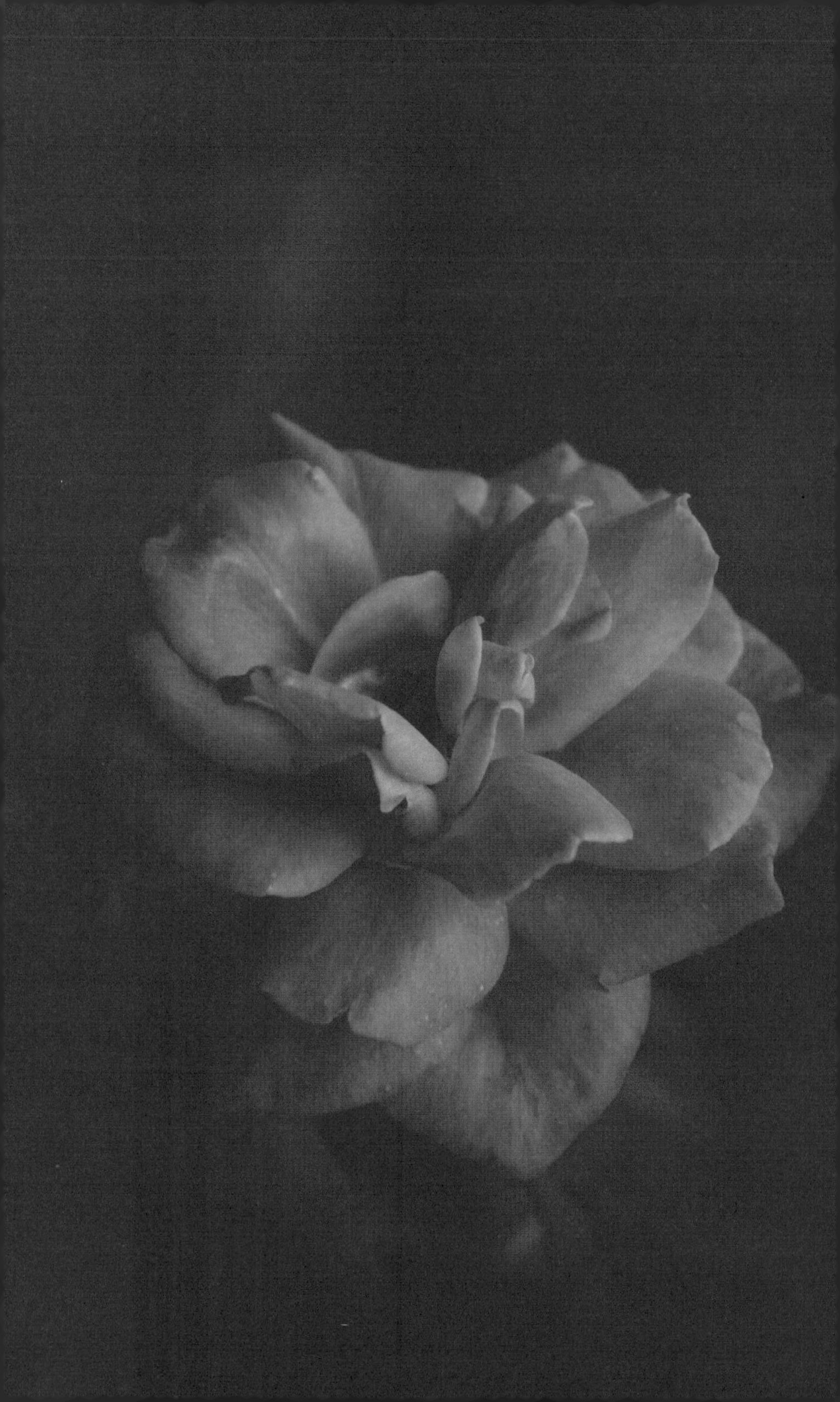

# IT'S ALREADY IN MOTION

Where you are right now didn't just start with you. It began with what God set in motion with someone before you. Somewhere a teacher, parent, grandparent, or friend placed a seed inside you, and that seed was waiting for the moment it could produce fruit so it could start a revolution inside of you.

Those who led the civil rights movement knew their cause was bigger than them and that if they were able to accomplish what was inside of them, it would change everything that came after them.

The same is true for you as you embark on this journey. This is bigger than you. This is about what you're going to set in motion on Earth.

Where do you want to see breakthroughs in your way of living, thinking, believing, giving, and receiving? I'm praying that God would highlight the area where He has ordained you to win. Pause, now, to name the breakthroughs you believe God can give.

| I WANT TO SEE THESE SPECIFIC BREAKTHROUGHS IN MY . . . | |
|---|---|
| Living | |
| Thinking | |

| | |
|---|---|
| Believing | |
| Giving | |
| Receiving | |

## ACCESS GOD'S HELP

Whether you requested it or not, you've likely received both criticism and correction from parents, supervisors, and others. Ideally, you were able to profit from their feedback.

Have you opened your heart to receive correction from the Lord? Depending on the spiritual tradition in which you were nurtured, you may not have considered or valued God's correction as being useful. But Scripture affirms, "The Lord disciplines the one he loves" (Hebrews 12:6 NIV). So as you pray, open your heart to receive God's correction.

## HOW TO PRAY

Close your eyes and quiet your heart. Spend a few minutes in silence, preparing to receive from the Lord. When you feel still before Him, invite God to show you the particular areas of your life where you can grow from correction.

- God, I am open to correction in my living.
- God, I am open to correction in my thinking.
- God, I am open to correction in my believing.
- God, I am open to correction in my giving.
- God, I am open to correction in my receiving.

## INSPIRATION

I believe that in every woman is an Eve and a Mary. There's a version of us who knows better but doesn't always do better. Then there's a version of us who has enough faith to say yes to whatever God asks her to do. A version of both women lives inside us all.

There will be some days when you know what you should do, but you are not going to be excited about it. Those are the days when Eve may be having her way in your life. Then there will be other days when you find the beauty in saying yes. Moments when you are so overwhelmed by what God has trusted you with that all you can do is sit back and take it all in. Those days, when your life is surrounded by the majesty of God, are the days when you look most like Mary.

### A Note from Sarah

This is *not* a race to finish an assignment! If you need to stretch this exercise out over more than one sitting, take your time. For example, today you might focus only on listening for God's correction in your living. Offer God your unhurried heart.

# MY PRAYER FOR YOU TODAY

*God, my sister is intent on making Your plan for her life a reality. Teach her to obey whatever word You have spoken over her. When she faces setbacks, inspire her to overcome and keep working to reach her goals. Give her the courage and strength to exercise the kind of discipline that will equip her to move forward. And when she is corrected, by You or by others, help her to receive that word with grace and implement it with wisdom. Amen.*

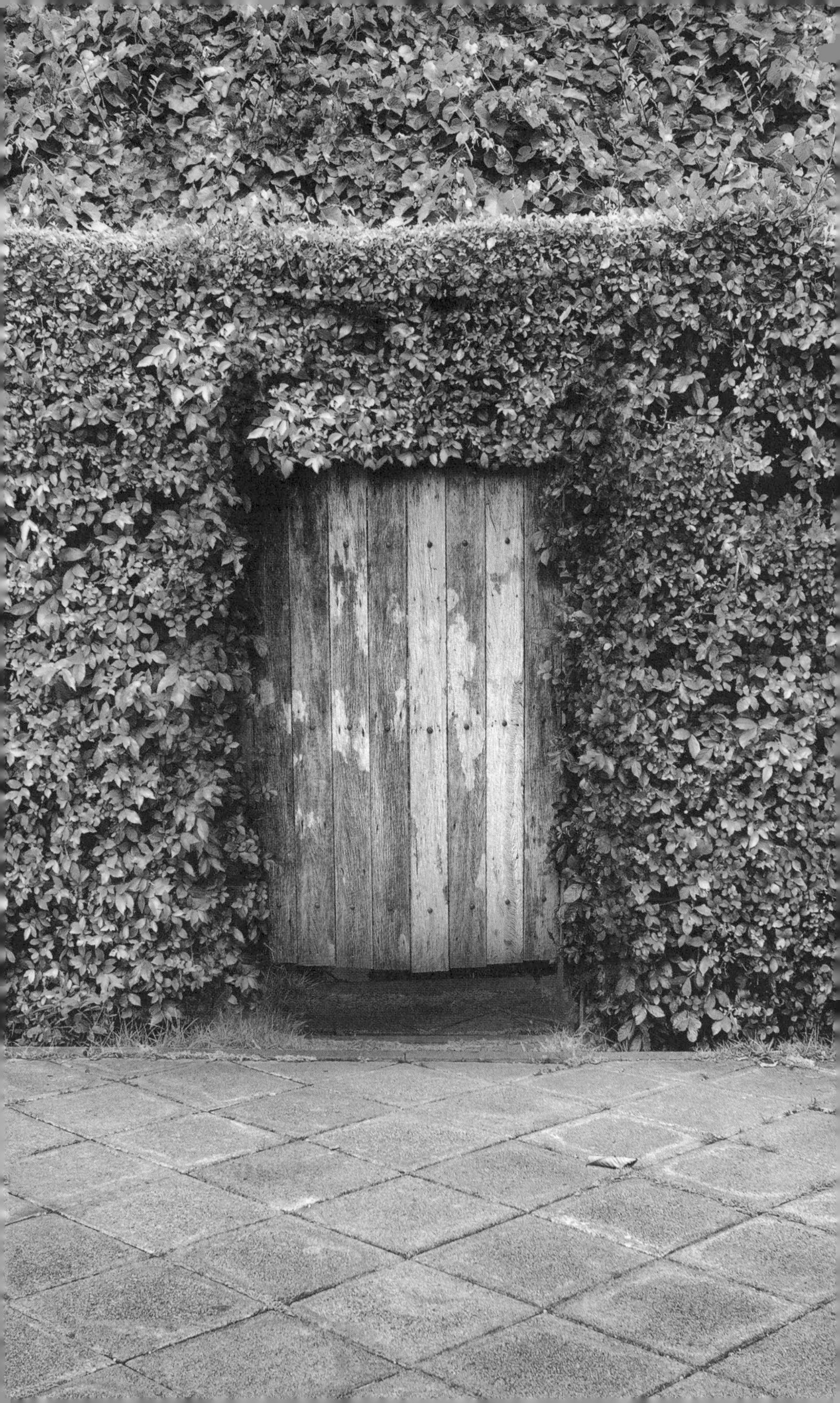

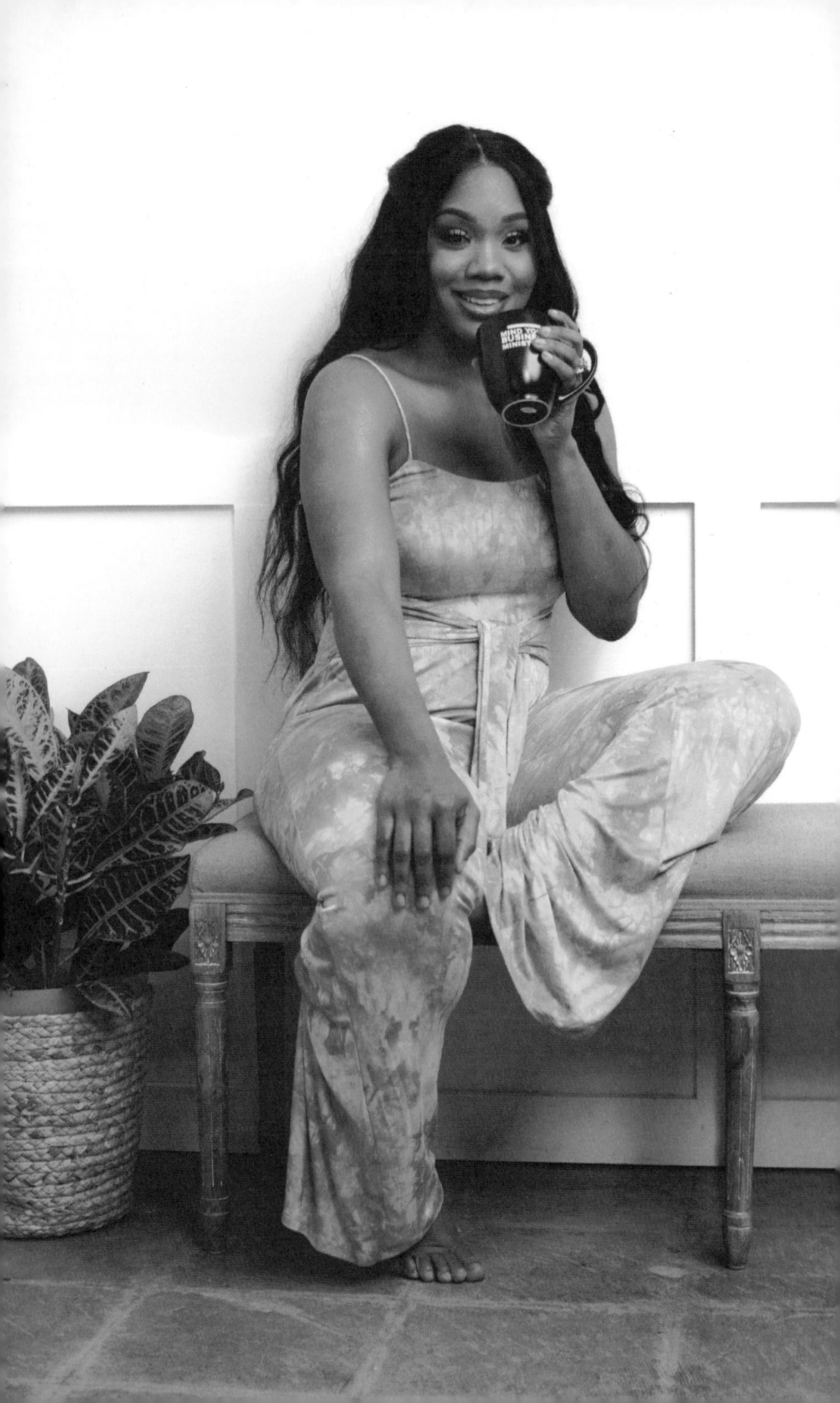

# CHAPTER TEN

# DON'T DO IT ALONE

*Blessed is she who believed, for there will be a fulfillment of those things which were told her from the Lord.*

—LUKE 1:45

I want to bring you to a place of great expectation. I want to give you permission to expect beauty out of life again. I'm praying that you would begin to believe that greater is coming *and* that you're worthy of receiving it.

It's hard to believe that we're worthy of greater when our actions have caused us to believe that not only are we not worthy but, because of our history, we cannot trust ourselves either.

When you look back over your life and you see moments when you expected better, but better didn't come, you learned to no longer trust your own heart. When you pursued a plan for which you were passionate, but the plan didn't turn out as you'd hoped, it trained you to not trust your passion. You can trust God with all of your heart; the true question is, can you learn to trust your heart again even after you've given it to God?

Trusting God with "all your heart" (Matthew 22:37) is trusting God with the entirety of your heart and all that it possesses. When you turn your heart over to God after it's been damaged, wounded, and abused, it's because it needs surgery. It's not because your heart needs to be tucked away in a safe. God brings your heart to a place of healing, perspective, and restoration, then He gives you your heart back and says, "Woman, evolve! You can trust who you're becoming because you trusted Me with your becoming."

## SOME EVE, SOME MARY

When I was pregnant, depressed, divorced, and distressed, God was there waiting for me to figure out who I was so I could walk into this moment when He trusted me to carry His glory. I only saw myself as Eve, but God saw me as Mary.

Today, what are the ways you see yourself as Eve? Where do you dwell on your sin, your shame, your mistakes, your failure? Be as honest as you can with yourself. When you expose these, you take a sledgehammer to the power they have over you!

_____

_____

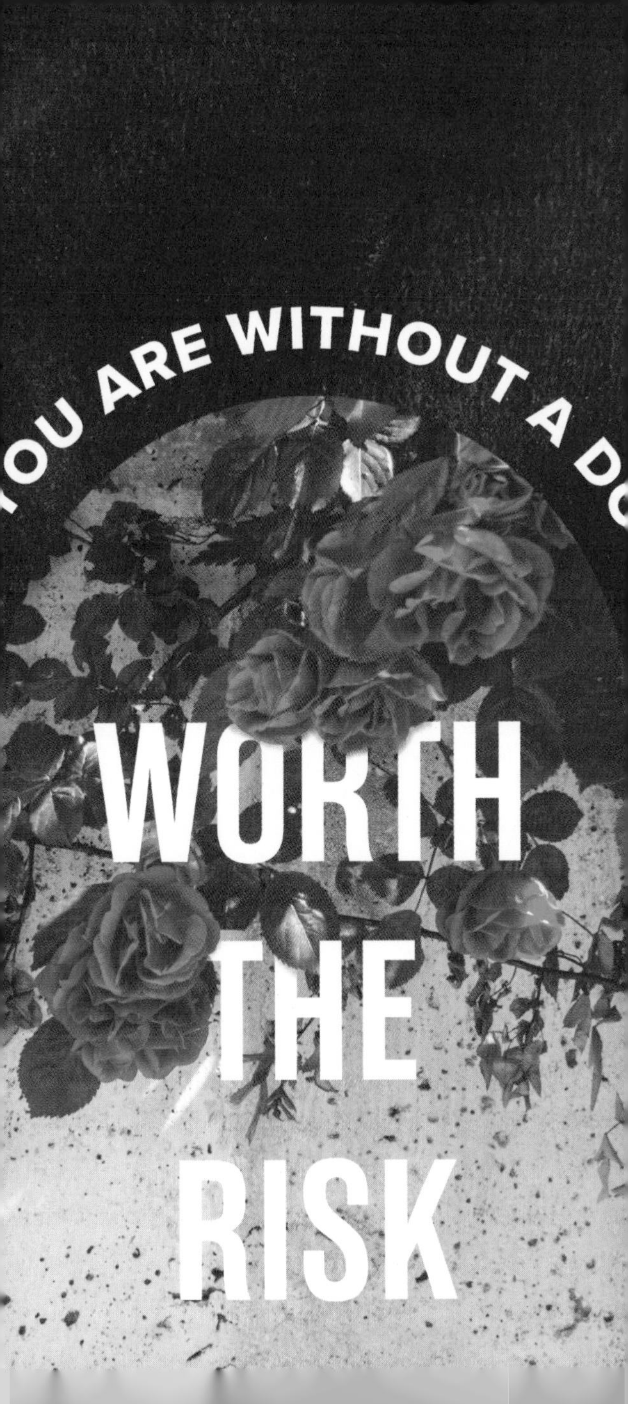
ARE WITHOUT A
WORTH
THE
RISK

_____

_____

_____

Today, what are the ways you see yourself as Mary? How do you recognize that you are God's chosen one who is blessed and highly favored?

_____

_____

_____

_____

## A FAVORED WOMAN AMONG FAVORED WOMEN

When Mary finally surrendered to the favor, she didn't just sit in the place where the angel met her; she went to find her cousin Elizabeth, who was pregnant with John (Luke 1:39–45). Why? Because favored women need other favored women. You have got to get in community with other women who see you worthy of celebration, not competition.

Today, are you part of a community of women who know themselves to be favored by God?

_____

_____

_____

_____

_____

If your answer is no, who is one woman toward whom you can move in friendship?

_____

_____

_____

_____

## CELEBRATING THE GIFTS OF OTHER WOMEN

You may be the champion your community needs. You can become the cheerleader in the corner of every woman pursuing her goal and not just of the women you prefer.

List the names of the first three women who come to mind. It doesn't matter how random they are or what your relationship is like. I'm not asking you to write down the names of women you respect or admire but, literally, just the first three names that come to mind.

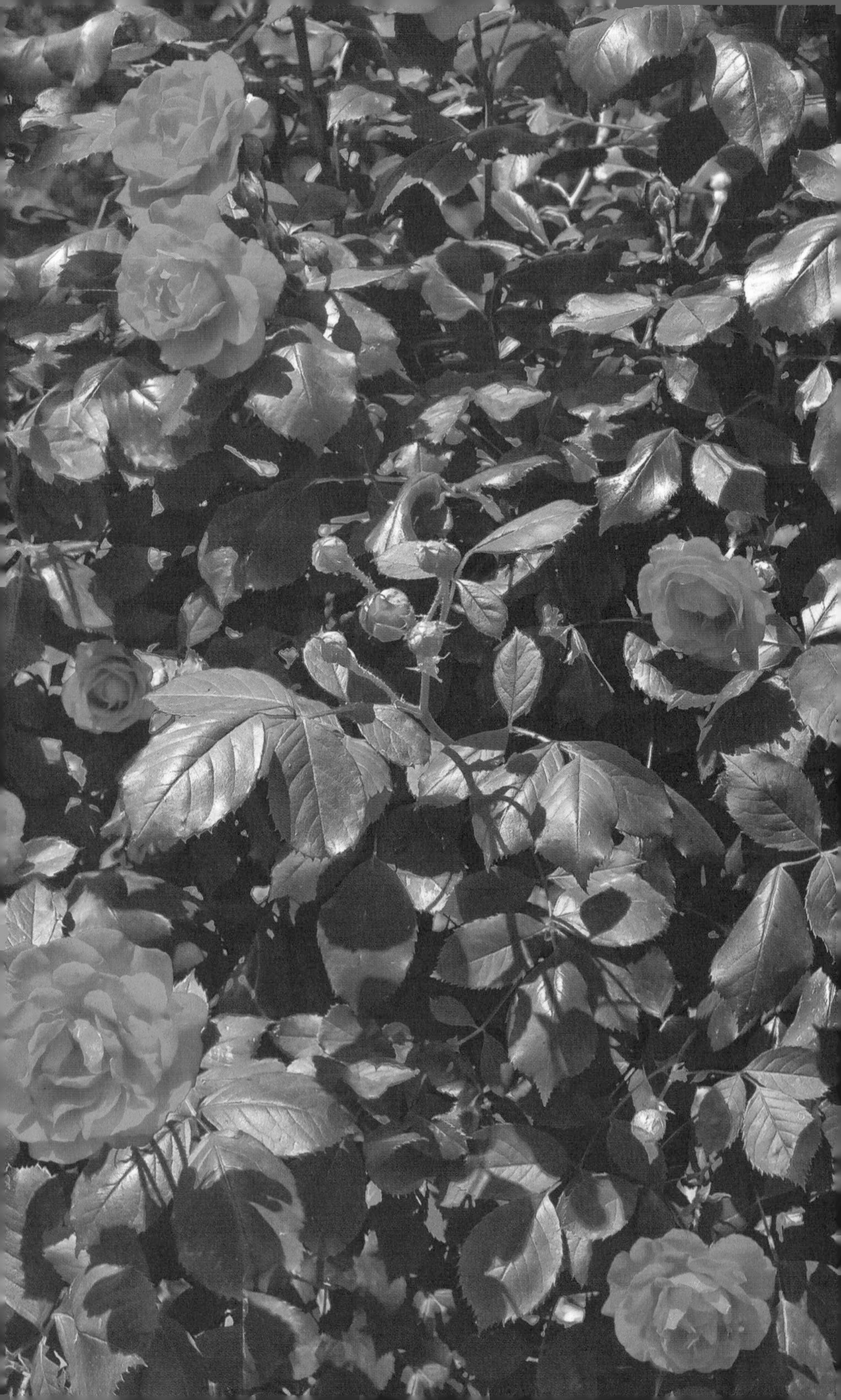

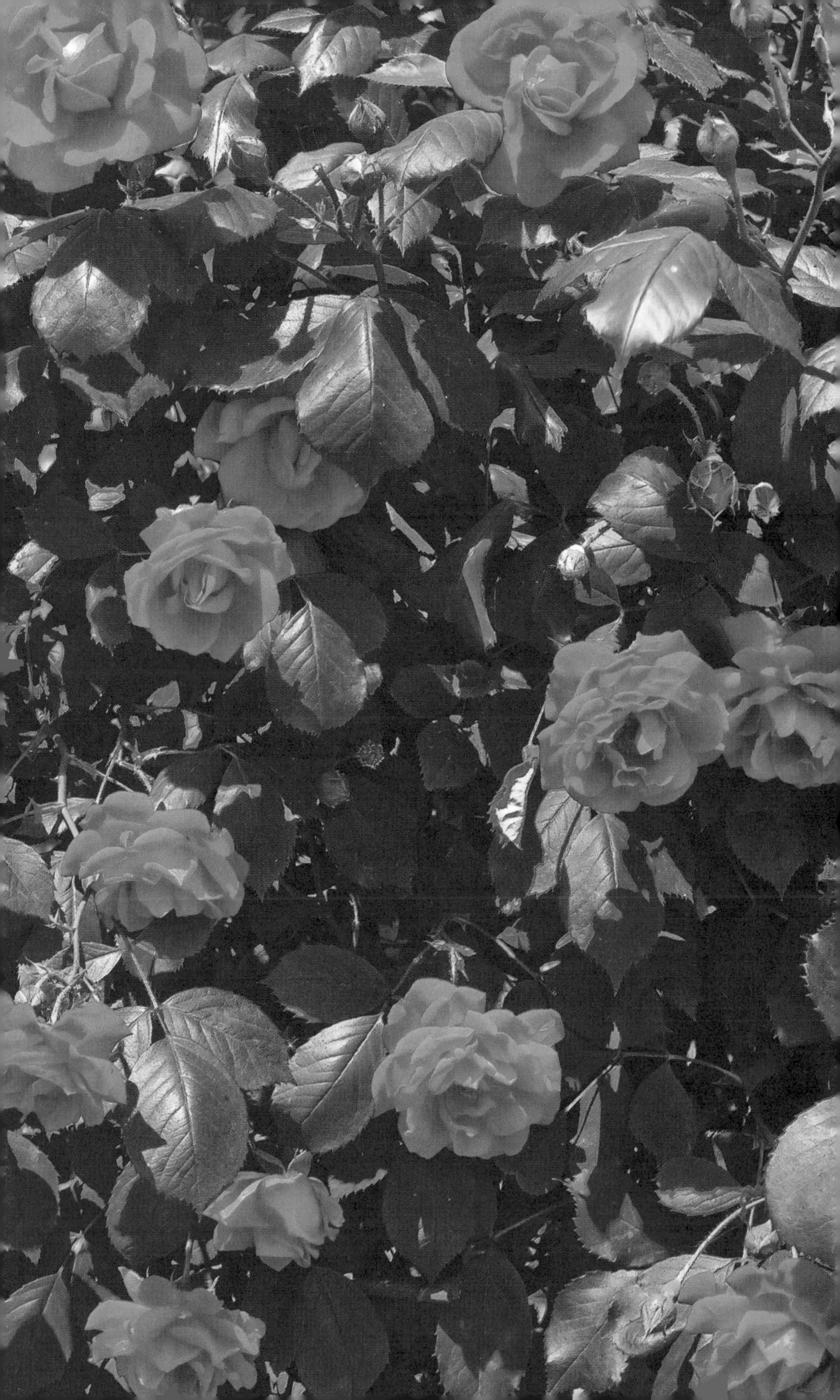

_____

_____

_____

Now write down one thing you feel each is gifted to do really well. It can be the way they speak, dress, love, support, build, or save. (Let the essence of each woman speak to your heart!)

_____

_____

_____

_____

_____

_____

Once you've done that, consider whether they realize the amazing gifts they have.

_____

_____

_____

_____

_____

Whether the answer is "I'm sure they know," or "I don't think they have a clue," I want you to understand the power God has given you to affirm another woman in what God has given her.

Finally, pause right now to phone, text, or email one woman on your list to affirm the particular gift or gifts God has given her.

Person I affirmed: _____

How I contacted her: _____

Gifting for which I affirmed her: _____

Continue to keep a list—here or on your phone—of each woman you intentionally affirm!

## ACCESS GOD'S HELP

In case you haven't figured it out, a lot of this journey to evolve happens in our heads! Our stuckness or our evolution depends on what we believe in our minds and the way those "stories" move us to action.

## HOW TO PRAY

If you've been believing a story that isn't true—that you're not worthy, that you're not prepared, that you're not equipped, that you're not able—invite God to transform your mind.

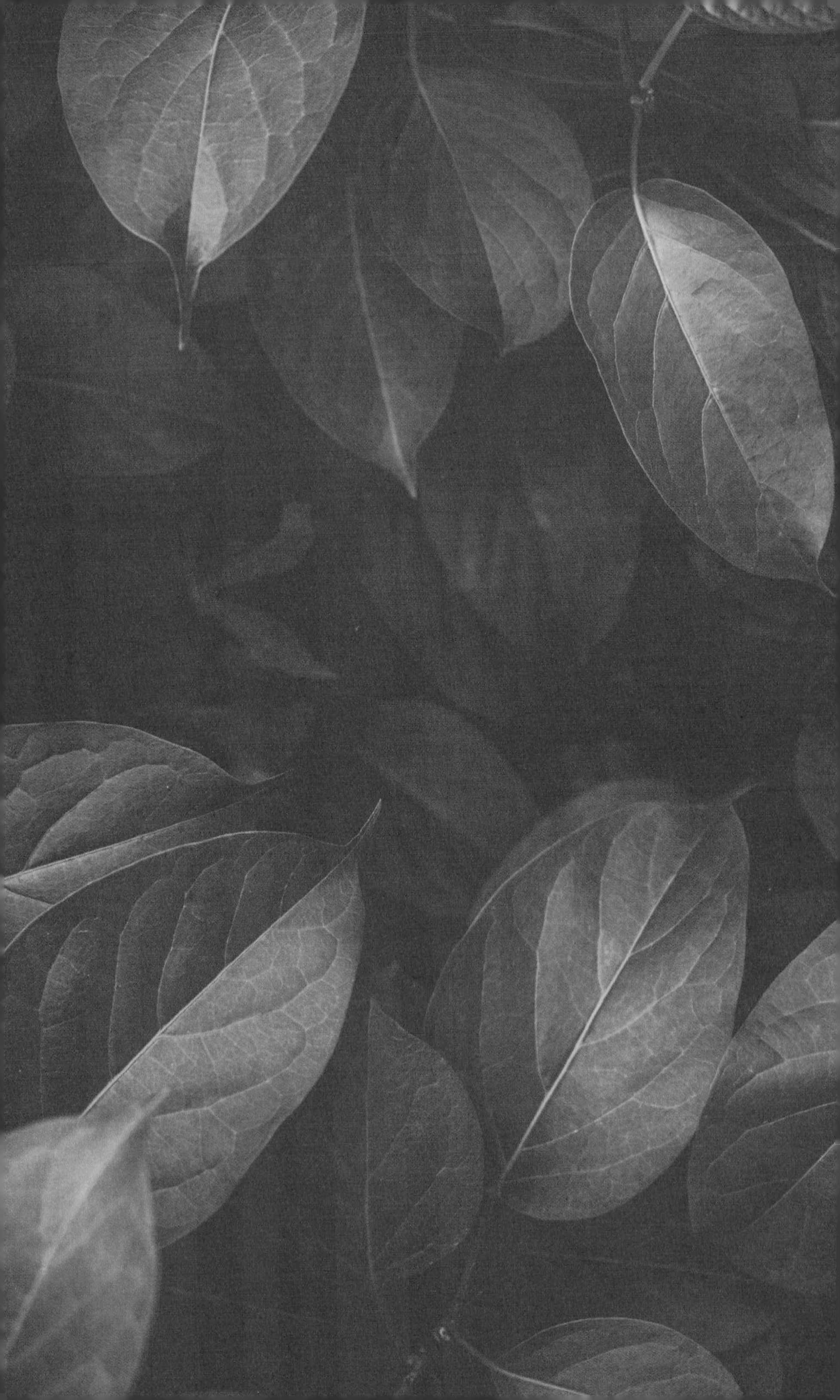

- God, expose my negative thinking and show me the false narrative about who I am that You are asking me to release.
- God, reveal the new narrative about who I am—and who You are!—that You are asking me to embrace.
- God, equip me to be the woman who celebrates the gifts of others. Bring to my mind the faces of those women who are preferred by me, and those who I don't often notice, that You are calling me to celebrate and affirm (jot each name down as you see her face).

_____

_____

_____

_____

_____

After you pray these prayers above, thank God for the insights He's granted you and commit to continuing to listen for the voice of the Holy Spirit who both speaks what is true and also nudges you to action as you bless the women God loves.

## INSPIRATION

Imagine if you took on the responsibility of not just becoming someone worthy of being honored and admired but becoming the kind of woman who makes other women feel honored and valuable too. That may require you to not allow your pride or ego to walk in the room before you do. Even so, I guarantee you will never lose when celebrating another woman's success. If you had to, you could go at this alone, but it would be a terrible injustice if you robbed another woman of the support and encouragement that could push her to the next dimension. Whether it's a stranger on the street or a lifelong relationship, create an opportunity to celebrate the strength of the women God allows you to cross paths with.

### A Note from Sarah

To embrace the reality that you are blessed among women, you have to break out of the mentality of thinking you're ordinary. That doesn't mean other women aren't blessed. It means that you have been blessed among women who have also been blessed in their own ways.

## MY PRAYER FOR YOU TODAY

*Father, I ask You to flood my sister's heart with great expectation. Help her to expect beauty out of life again. Convince her that greater is coming and that she's worthy of receiving it! Silence the voice of the Enemy in her life that accuses her of not being worthy. Teach her to trust You with her whole heart and all that it possesses. And as she trusts You, grant her the healing, perspective, and restoration You have for her, in the strong name of Jesus. Amen.*

———————

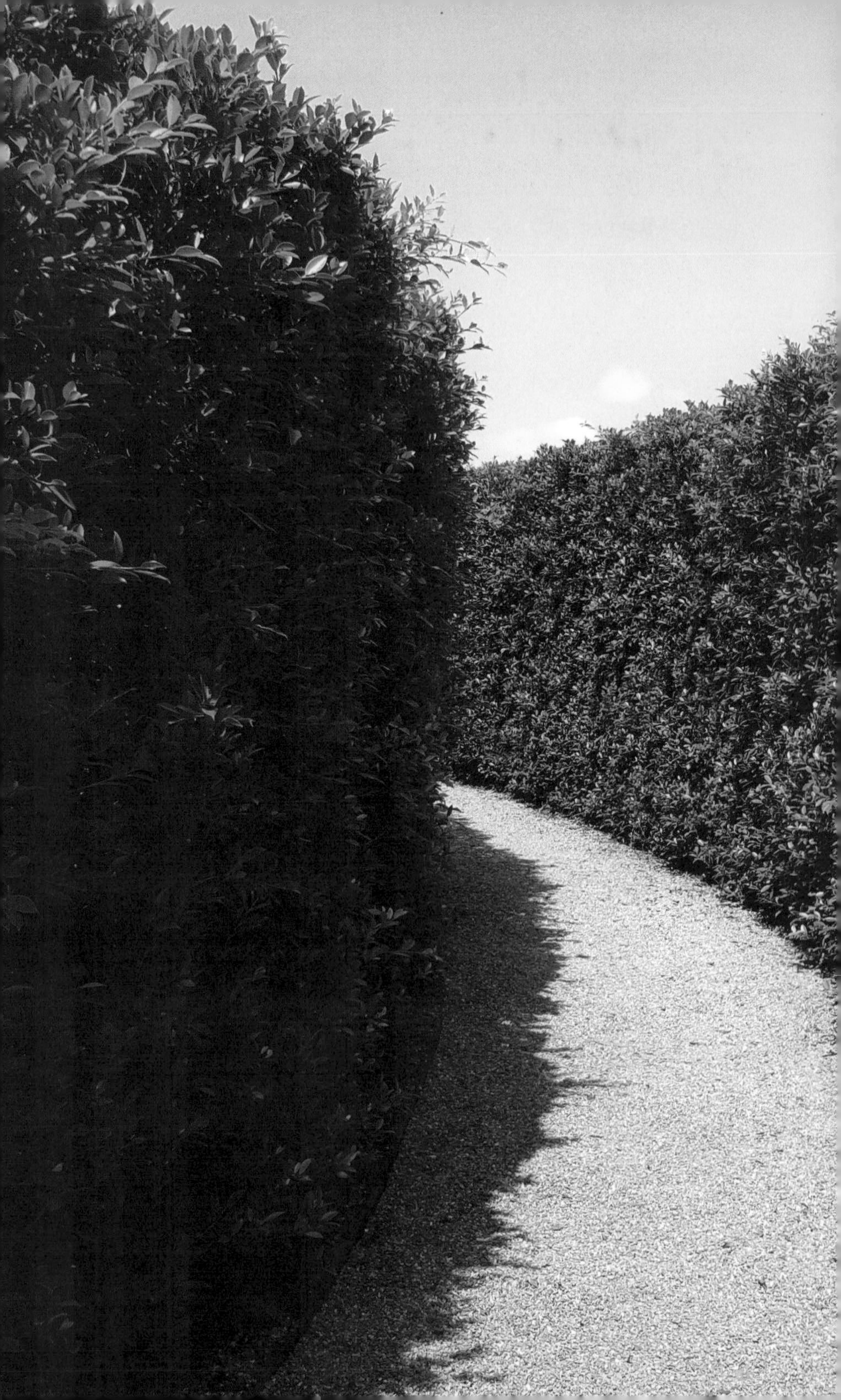

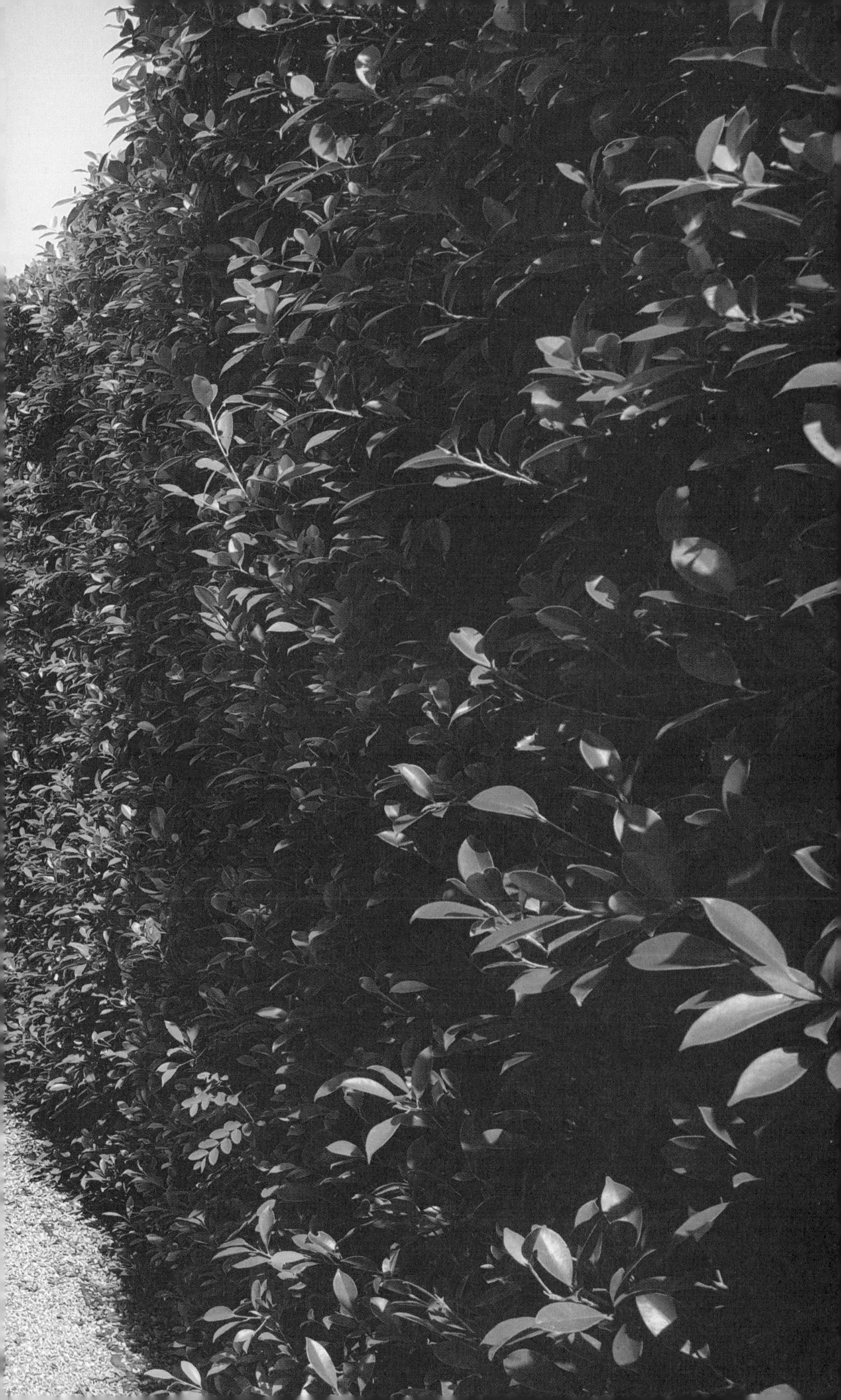

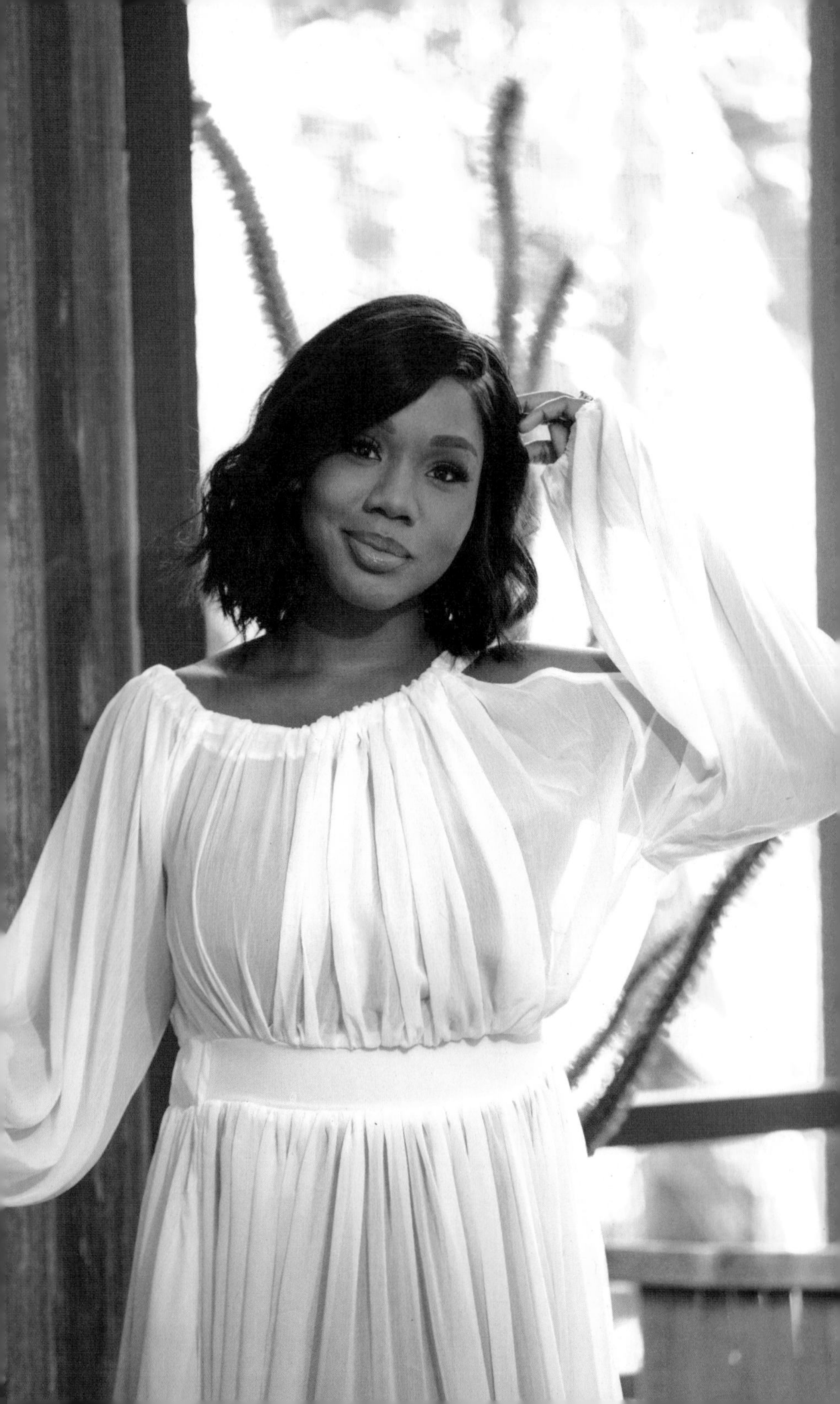

# CHAPTER ELEVEN

# WILD WOMAN

> *"I make known the end from the beginning,*
> *from ancient times, what is still to come.*
> *I say, 'My purpose will stand,*
> *and I will do all that I please.'"*
> **—ISAIAH 46:10 NIV**

You know the mighty women of faith in the Bible: Ruth, Deborah, Esther, Mary. Sometimes I wonder if my disconnect with the Bible reflected my not being able to see myself. So often I felt unsure of myself and my faith in comparison to the more popular women we've come to celebrate. All that changed when I had a chance to study Eve. She is the mother of all humankind and the mother of every woman.

As you seek to take up your space in your world, you must never forget the value of representation. To see glimpses of yourself in Scripture and to watch God's faithfulness to that person is to understand how God can connect with you now.

It is equally important that you recognize you are someone else's representation.

As a black woman, I understand how lack of representation can limit your ability to gauge your potential. But while watching a documentary about Danny Trejo, a Latino-American actor, it dawned on me that lack of representation affects everyone. I'm telling you this because I think it's important you realize that you are someone else's mirror.

The footprints that led you to this moment are so similar to where someone is standing right now—they may never find their way if you don't become their guide. When you come to the realization of how interconnected we all are, you will recognize that your confinement does not affect just you; it also affects people you can't even see.

## RUN YOUR RACE

It's time for you to run your race, my friend. It's time for you to let the wind hit your face and wipe away your tears. It's time for you to unleash your faith and run away from the place of insecurity and inadequacy that threatens to devour your seed. God will most certainly meet you where you are, but God will never keep you where you are.

Sometimes we have to stop asking God to change our present and instead ask Him to unshackle us from the need to stay when we've been called to run our race.

As you prepare to run your race, ask God to show you

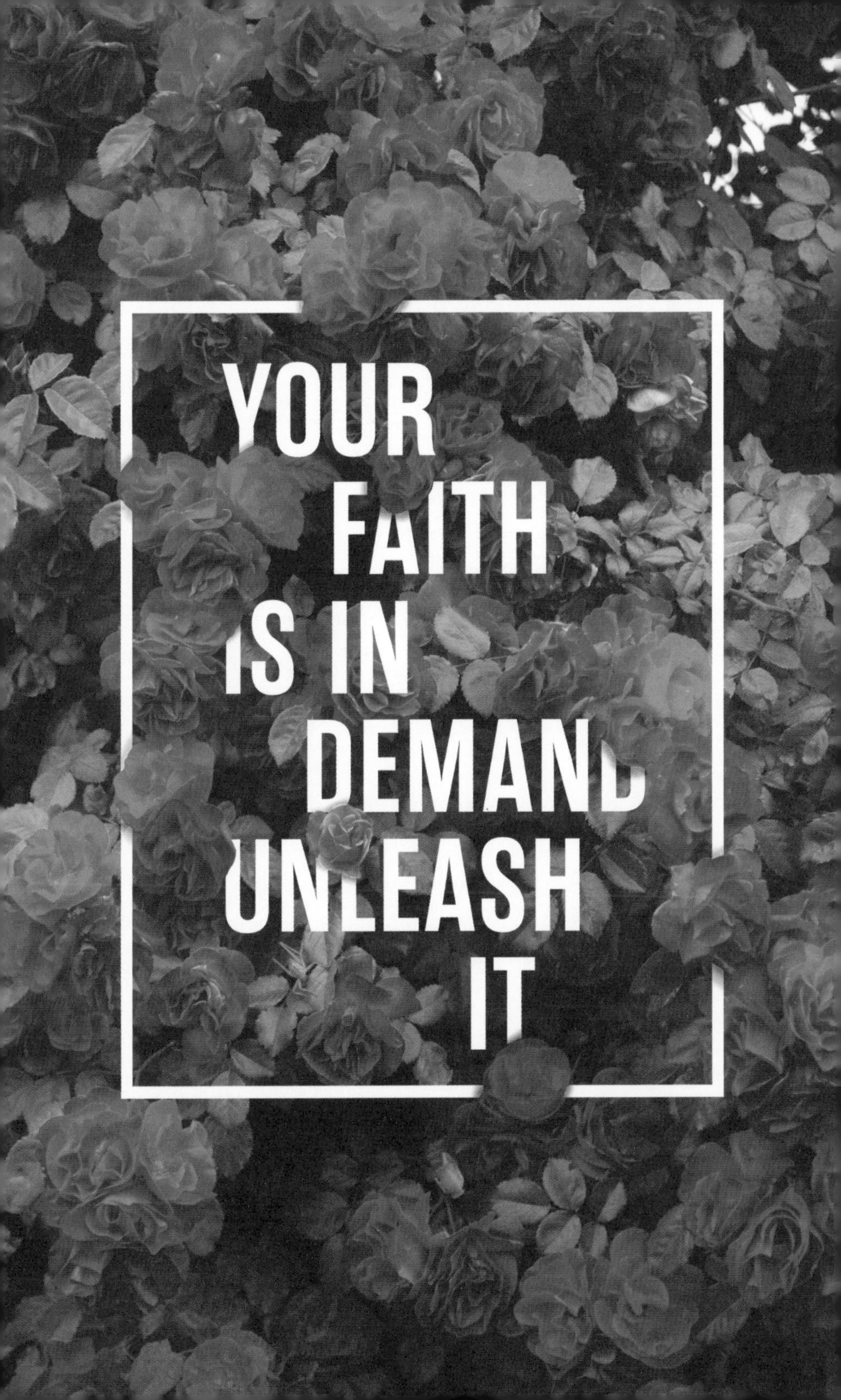
YOUR
FAITH
IS IN
DEMAND
UNLEASH
IT

the places where you are shackled today. When God reveals the places where you're still bound, set down this book, close your eyes, and ask God to *show you* how He is releasing you from your chains.

## WHERE'S YOUR WILDERNESS?

While we may not be headed into an actual wilderness, we have all been chosen to live in conditions not always hospitable to faith, purpose, creativity, innovation, vulnerability, and authenticity. I want to invite you to identify your wilderness.

## IDENTIFY YOUR WILDERNESS

For some, living in a space of vulnerability feels like being in a wilderness. For others, starting a business or going back to school feels like the wilderness. You may choose to stop advocating for everyone else and finally start looking at your own soul, and that feels wild.

You are being called to transition into a way of being that feels uncultivated, uninhabited, and inhospitable. Whatever your wilderness is, I want you to label it. What is that place?

_____

_____

## BENEFIT FROM YOUR WILDERNESS

Instead of bracing ourselves and waiting for the next wave of change, we are going to vow to become change.

Write down why your wilderness is important to your development.

_____

_____

_____

_____

_____

## STOP AND NOTICE

You're going to have these moments when you feel perfectly aligned with your Creator. When those moments come, I don't want you to bask in them without taking a moment to jot down your habits, routines, and thoughts.

Right now, take stock

### A Note from Sarah

As you head into your wilderness, you're not going to be the same woman. You'll be wiser, smarter, stronger, and more compassionate, empathetic, and confident because you dared to do something new.

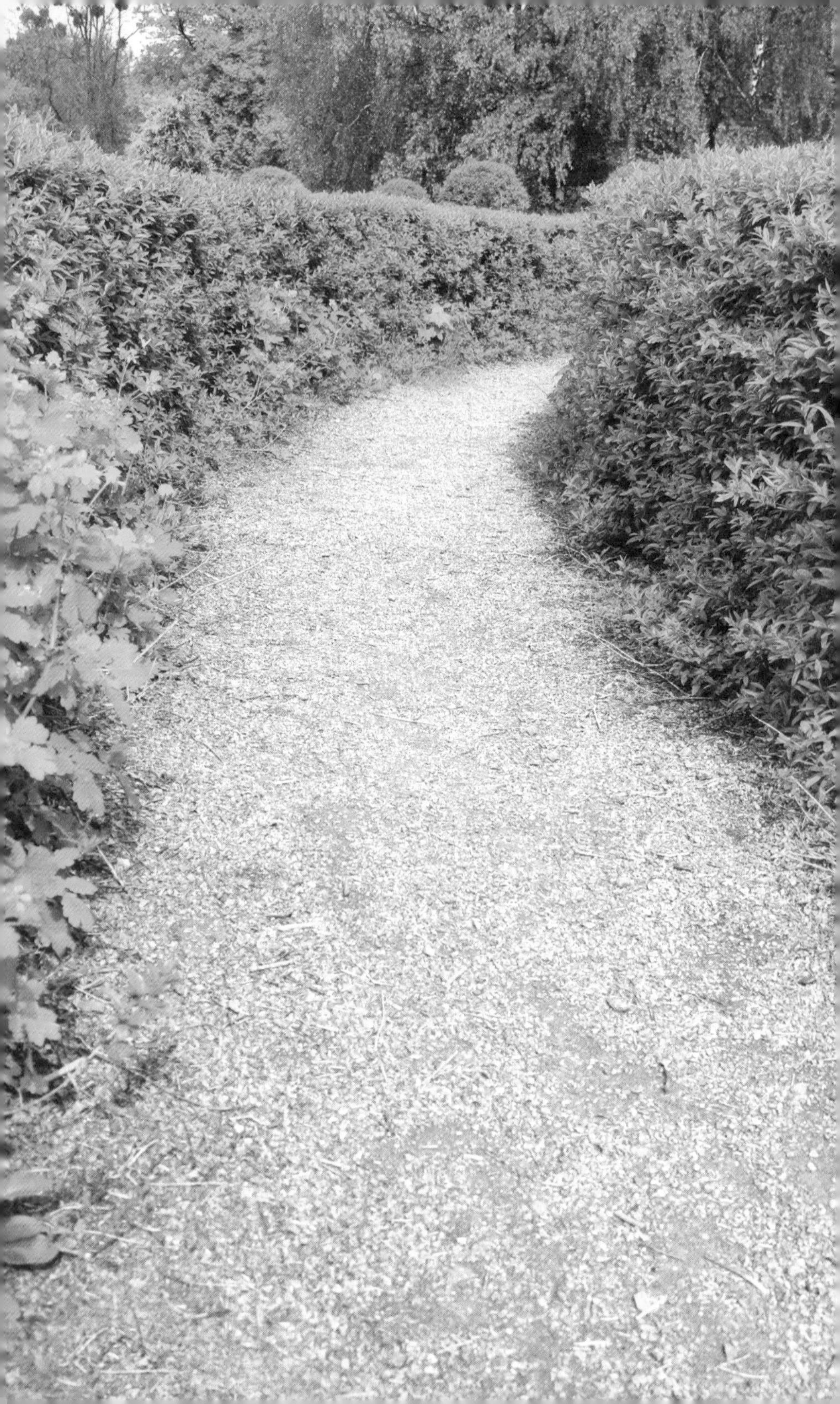

of the ways—up until now—that you have felt this sense of deep satisfaction. You're searching for those moments, or ventures, or experiences, or projects when

- you experienced peace,
- you felt joy,
- you were confident in the decisions you made,
- you were confident in the plans you were pursuing, and
- you felt aligned with God.

The times when I was aligned with my Creator because I was being the best version of myself were:

_____

_____

_____

_____

_____

As you glance over those experiences, can you identify any habits, routines, or thoughts that contributed to your success? Jot them down here.

_____

_____

_____

_____

_____

_____

_____

_____

## ACCESS GOD'S HELP

Friend, the end of this guide is just the beginning of your journey. When God created you He saw the woman that He destined you to become. My prayer throughout these pages has been that you, too, would catch that vision that your Maker has for you.

### A Note from Sarah

You need to mark the spots in your habits and routines that allow you to feel most aligned with the highest version of yourself. When you finally know where your place is, it gets easier and easier to return there. The hardest part of the journey is learning where home is for you, but once you know where home is, it can't be taken away from you. So continue to jot down these wins and what contributed to them!

We've covered a lot of ground together, haven't we? And that's why I want to carve out space, here, for you to pause and process with God all you've absorbed.

## HOW TO PRAY

Slowly take a deep, cleansing breath, and then release it. Do this three times.

Invite God to be in the home, the room, the space where you are.

As we conclude, be intentional about identifying and capturing the specific takeaway God has for you.

With a listening heart, pray:

*God, what is the* **one thing** *that You most want me to take away from the experience of reflecting on my life and what You have for me?*

(It might be a single word. It might be a Scripture passage. It might be an idea. Listen . . . )

_____

_____

_____

_____

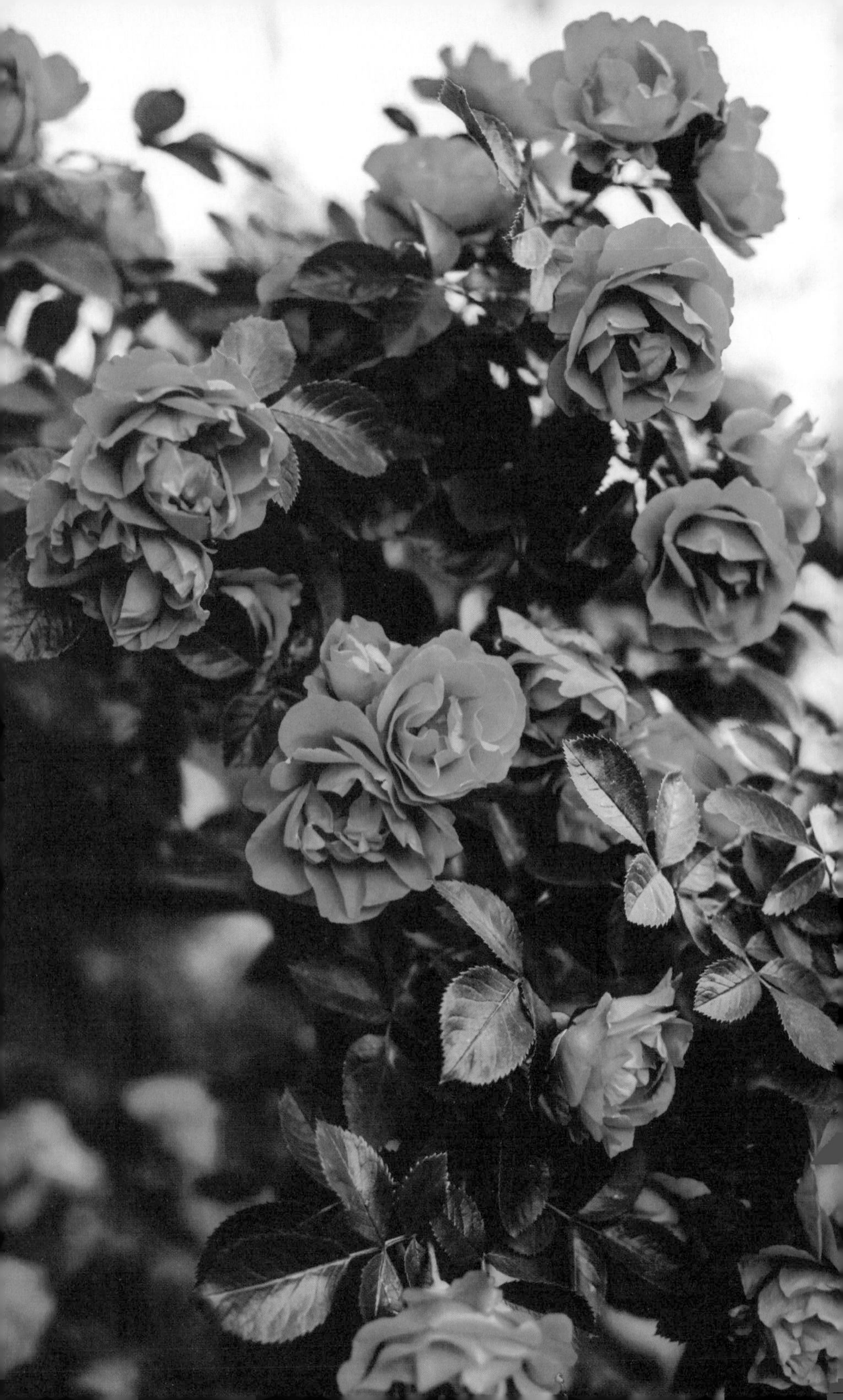

_____

_____

---

*And, Lord, what is the next thing You want me to do as I commit to becoming the woman You created me to be? What is my next step?*

---

_____

_____

_____

_____

_____

When you've identified the "one thing" and the "next thing," write them down on a piece of paper and tape them to your bathroom mirror. Hold them tight. Protect them. (And when you've accomplished your first "next thing," ask God again and replace the first "next" with the *next* "next"!)

## INSPIRATION

I want you to know that there's a place on the earth that has been reserved with your life in mind. Your destination hasn't been canceled nor has it been denied. You may have found your place once but somehow lost your way. That place is still yours, and because you're still here, there's an opportunity for you to get back to your place and experience the life God had in mind when He created you.

You already know that life may not be smooth sailing. There may be moments when it's downright tough, but being effective at the reason you were created is much more fulfilling than having a life that doesn't rock any boats.

Girl, the mere fact that you've dug deep and reflected on your life in this guided journal is a sign that you don't mind putting in the work. You're ready. You're more ready than you've ever been.

## MY PRAYER FOR YOU TODAY

*Good and faithful Father, I offer my sister to You in this moment, with the confidence that You are setting her free from feelings of stuckness, unworthiness, and uncertainty to become the version of herself You created her to be. Heal her heart and transform her mind. God, I thank You in advance that generations will be changed because she assumed her mission. I trust that You are carrying her in Your heart and enveloping her with Your love and power. Amen.*

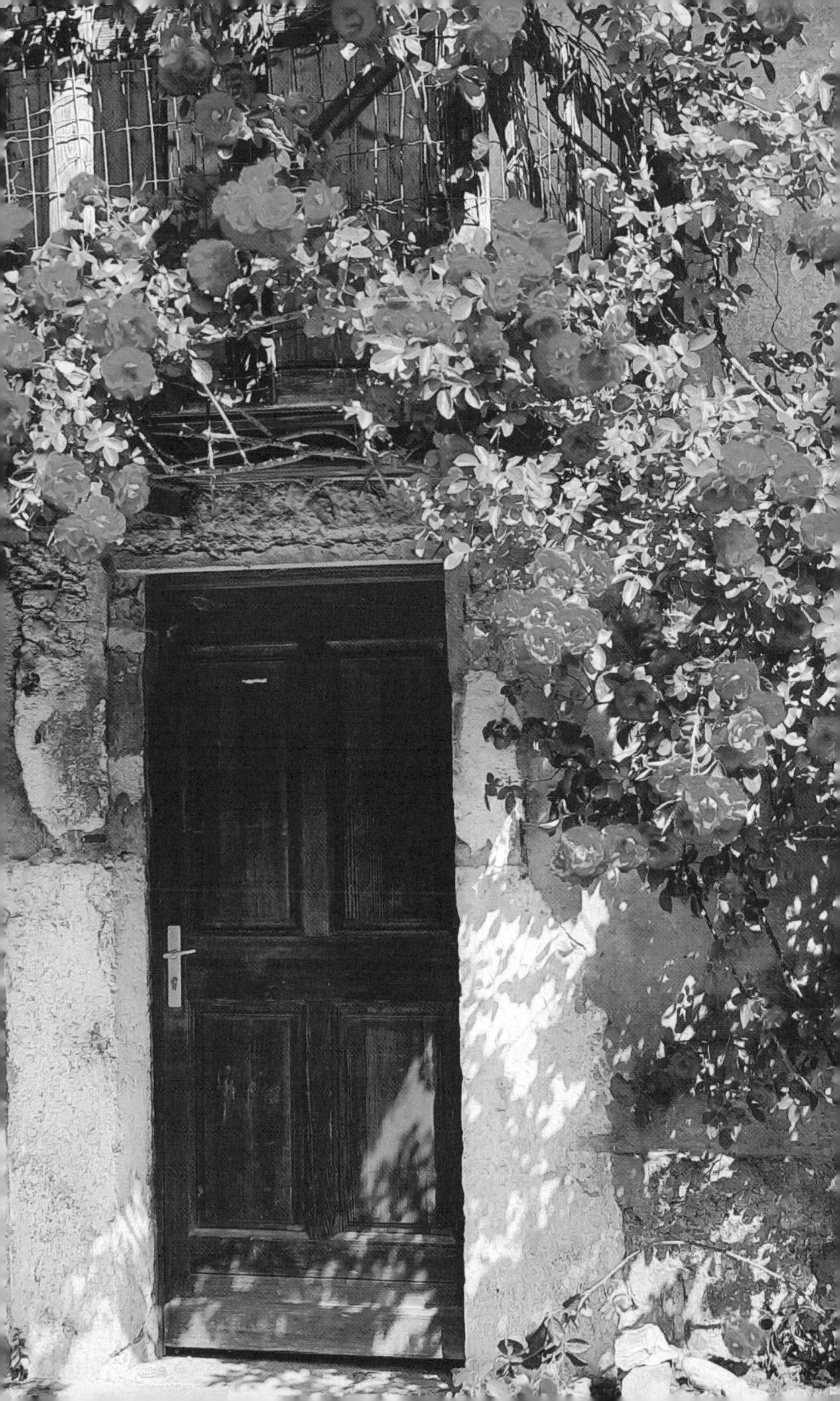

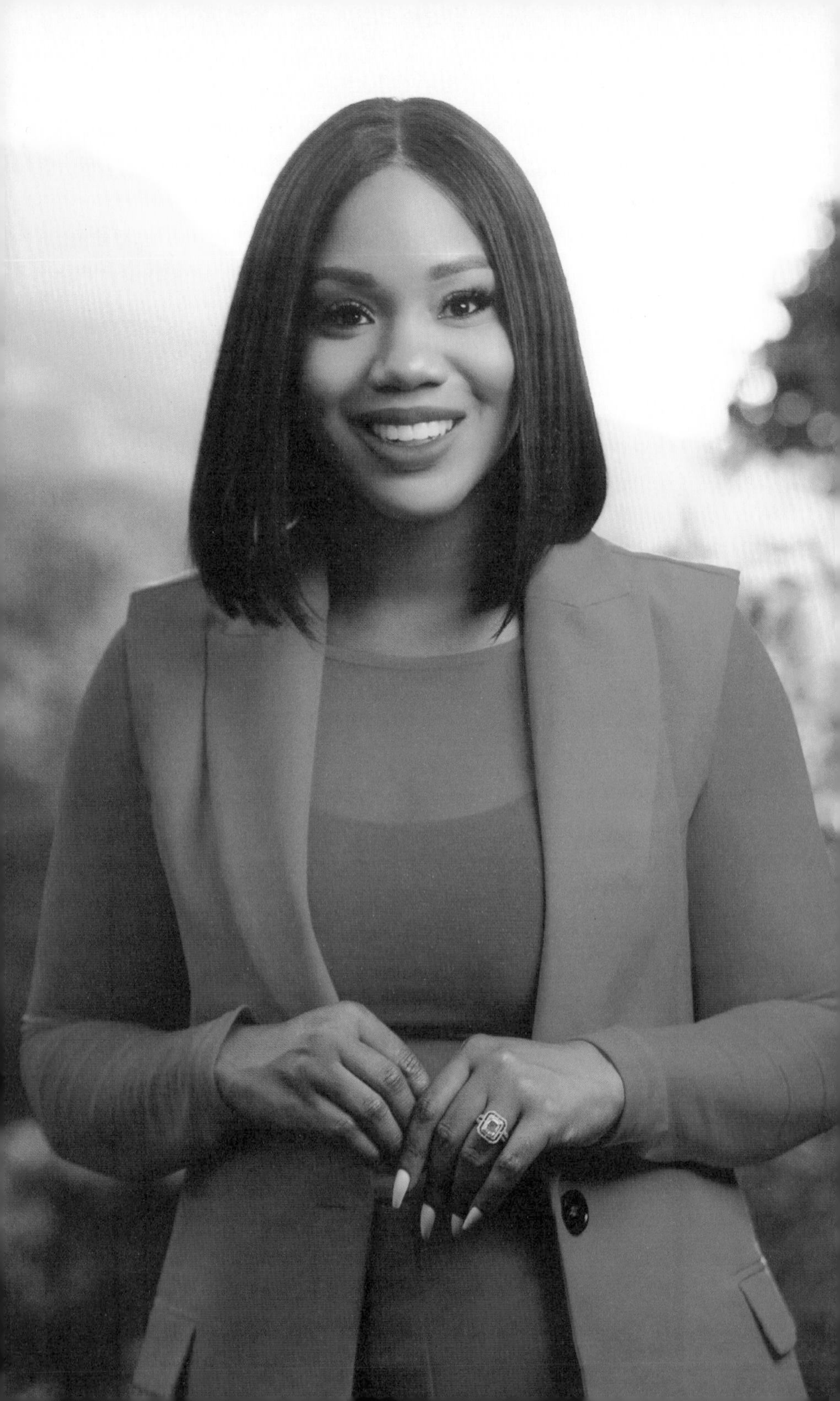

# ABOUT THE AUTHOR

Sarah Jakes Roberts is the founder of Woman Evolve, best-selling author, and media personality who strives to balance career, ministry, and family. She has been the driving force behind grassroots marketing for films, publications, and community programs that inspire and uplift people of all ages and backgrounds. Sarah is the daughter of Bishop T.D. Jakes and Mrs. Serita Jakes and pastors a dynamic community of artists and professionals in Hollywood alongside her husband, Touré Roberts. Together they have six beautiful children and reside in Los Angeles.

# YOU DON'T HAVE TO LIVE YOUR FUTURE DEFINED BY YOUR PAST.

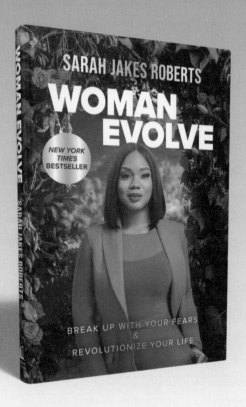

ISBN 978-0-7852-3554-5

Available wherever books are sold

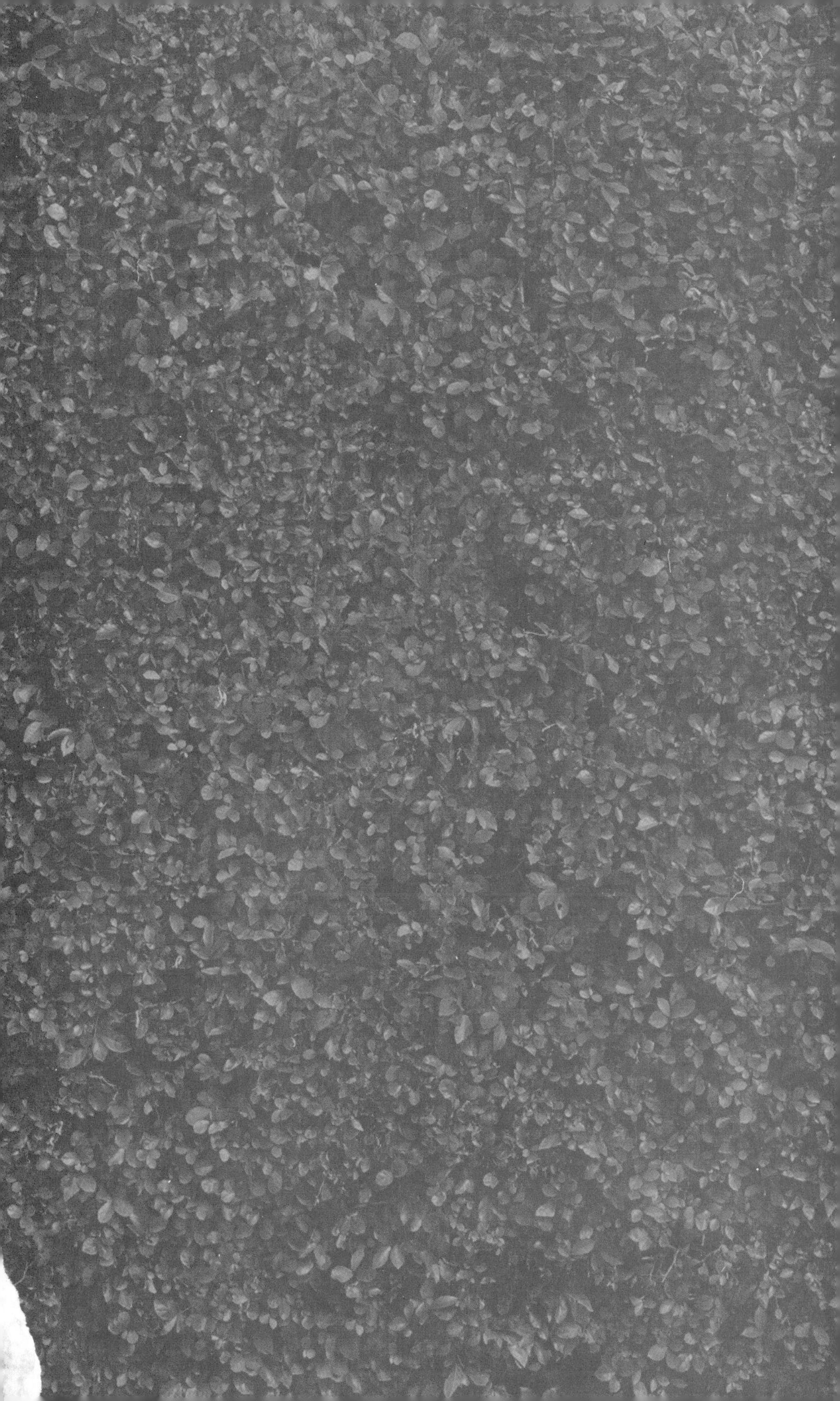

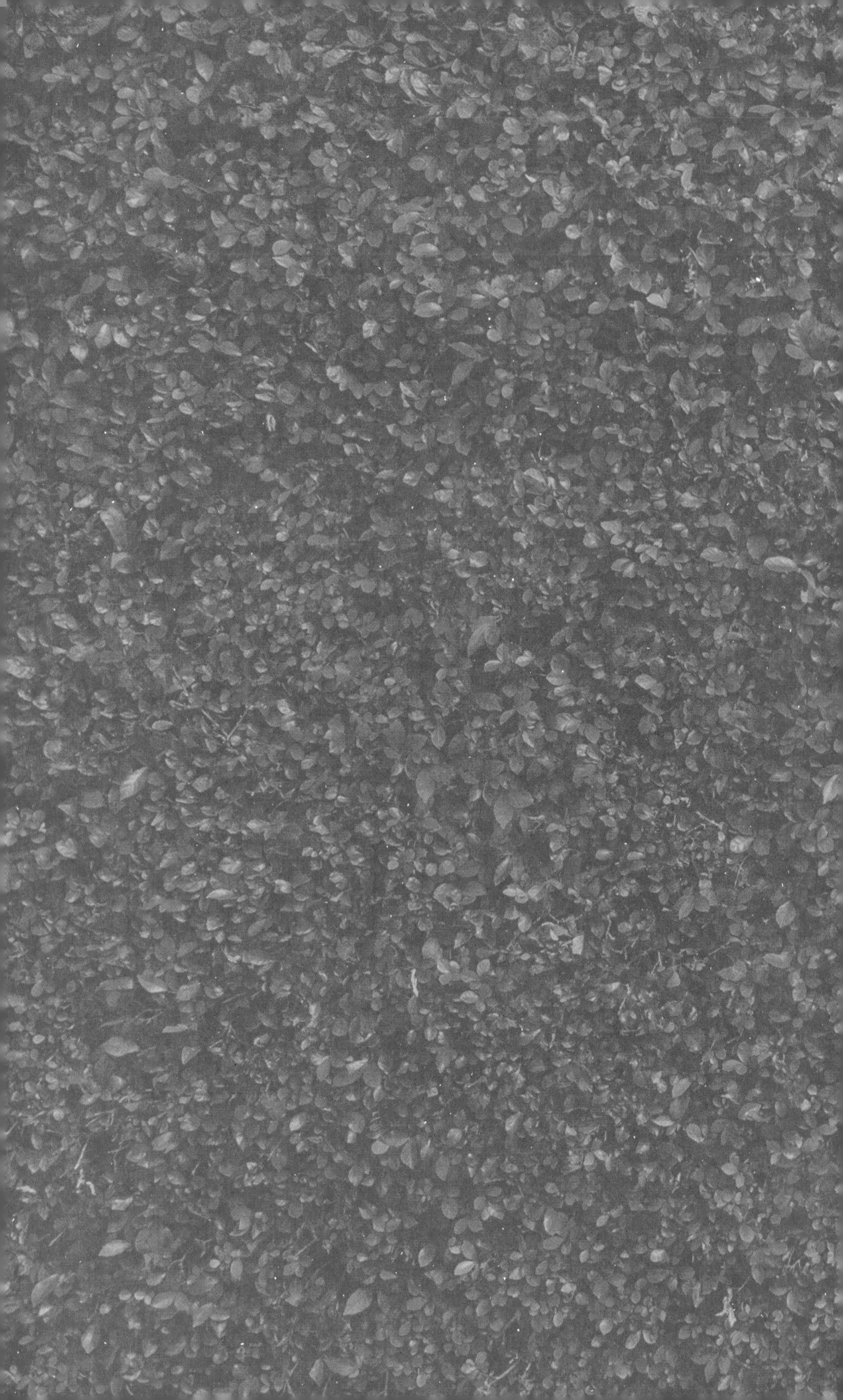